Just Lucky I Guess

Just Lucky I Guess

Tom Stern

© 2018 Tom Stern
All rights reserved.
Cover Design by Couris Group

Photo from LIFE Magazine
(First Paid Job in Showbiz
Story on Pg. 103)

ISBN: 1977751431
ISBN 13: 9781977751430

Preface

Annoyed is probably the best way to describe how I feel about the realization that I didn't know much about my Mom or my Dad…why not?…I just don't remember either my father or my mother discussing their childhood or their parents or their schools or anything remotely intimate.

Actually it was Jenna that got me thinking awhile ago when she brought up the fact that she or Nicolas didn't know much about me so I wrote 'Smatterings of Dad', a kind of random samplings of my life but it just wasn't easy to read…

So, this year Jenna said that Calla wanted to know about my childhood and I wrote the story that starts this book of short stories about my life.

When I finished writing this, I realized I liked this format because it felt like I was telling rather than writing the story.

I immediately started a list of titles that would be the stories I would like to tell.

And the short-story became my way of writing this book.

As I wrote these stories, I realized surely everyone has a book of short stories in them…and I am convinced the very reasons I wrote this book apply to most people who might read this, so I encourage you all to start writing because your family and their future families are, in fact, interested.

My children's children's children will know who the 'Papa' is/was.

CHAPTERS

Preface ································· v

Childhood at the Jersey Shore ············· 1
Being Jewish ························· 8
The Rooster ·························· 17
Monmouth Park ······················· 25
My Magic Bat ························ 28
My Passion ·························· 32
Dodgers ····························· 37
New Years Eve 55' ···················· 39
We have a Drink Together ·············· 42
You're in the Army Now! ··············· 48
Never Volunteer ······················ 54
Korea or Germany····················· 58
Frankfurt ···························· 61
Game On! ···························· 64
Baseball in Germany ·················· 71
The Dilemma ························· 74
The Shit Hits the Fan ················· 78
Springtime in Europe ················· 81

The Last Hurrah	86
Back from the Zone	89
Rain	93
A Close Call	96
My First Job	103
But He is George to Me!	107
The White Elephant	117
Road to Hollywood	121
Hallelujah Trail	126
Ahead of My Time	130
Horses	135
Ba in Film (So, You Want to Make a MOVIE?)	142
The Whole Shabang	158
Juana Boy	166
MBA in Film	172
Music	179
The Film	183
Charlie	188
Summers	191
Fat Boy	200
Nickerson Housing Development AKA The Nick	206
DMV	211
84'Olympics	214
Peeeeench!!	224
Fire on the Beach	233
Da Big Board Break	239
Sundays	247
To Be Continued	256

Childhood at the Jersey Shore

Nine days after my birth I was moved to the only house I ever knew, 315 South Lincoln Ave…Elberon, NJ and I am sure you have no idea where this is…but it is on the Jersey Shore, just north of Asbury Park and halfway between Asbury Park and Long Branch, the home of Max's, the best hot dog on earth, according to all that have tasted it.

Anyway, I think you will have a hard time finding many that lived in one home till they went away to college…it's a rarity.

I have no idea of the exact circumstances surrounding the buying of my home except that my mom (Ros) and dad (Harry) had just gone thru 'the depression of 29' and had to move…somewhere!

In November of 1932, two incredible things happened…I was born and Franklin Delano Roosevelt became the President of the United States. He was to take the country out of the worst of times as the depression hit the country in 1929, and everything had changed. And not for the better.

The country experienced the worst economic collapse in its history…the stock market went bust…everyone lost everything and money became worthless…suicide rates jumped because the wage-earners didn't know how they were going to feed their families …things were bad!...you know the expression 'worth more dead than alive'. That applies here.

My father and his brothers were in the leather business which was flourishing before the crash, and everyone had lots of money. My dad had found this gorgeous gal named Rosalind Dreyfus and had been smitten with her. His first wife had died unexpectedly and he had a son named Hank who was 14 at the time of the marriage. Then, all of a sudden, the leather business went under.

Harry and Ros knew they could no longer live in the 'posh' Maplewood/South Oranges, so they decided to move to the Jersey Shore to the little town of Elberon, and somehow buy a house. There were no 'rentals' in those day and they probably paid less than $5,000 for the house, on payments of course because all their savings were gone.

Dad got a job working at Bamberger's, a well known department store in Newark, NJ.

He commuted every day from the Elberon train station, which was within walking distance on a nice day.

Mom took care of everything because women didn't work in those days. As a matter of fact, everyone had a 'helper' (housekeeper/cook/babysitter) and they slept upstairs in the attic. They worked for 'very little money plus room an board'. The house had three bedrooms and one bathroom on the second floor, and a bedroom/bath on the third. The house is still there!

My Mom and Dad loved the ocean, they loved the water. Dad fished from the beach and more importantly knew how to ride waves on his chest, so both my brother Hank and myself would go for early morning 'dips' in the summer with Dad and of course he taught me how to ride the waves…we used to go to the public beach at Phillips Ave in Deal, an upscale town just south of us.

Dad was a very good athlete and played amateur baseball as well as tennis and golf…I was told he could do anything with a racket…Mom played everything as well and was a very good golfer/tennis player…so at a very early age, I knew I was blessed with sports ability…and therefore…so are my kids and their kids!

All of Dad's friends commuted with him to either Newark or New York and they would play gin or bridge every day, to wile away the time…the commute each day took two hours each way…and I might add right here, that there was no air-conditioning, so when my Dad would come trudging home during the summer, his suit and tie were soaking wet.

My best memories of my older brother (17 years older) was that he went to MIT and had a model T Ford that he took completely apart in the garage and then put it back together. He took me over the many dirt roads that were behind all the small coastal towns. I could always make my brother laugh so we had fun!

Mom went into the real estate biz and Dad changed jobs and went to Wall Street as things were picking up…I was then at Oakhurst Grammar School which was a 'walk thru the woods' to school…there were no houses, just woods!...that would all change soon enough.

The Bycks lived next door in a large white-columned colonial house with a rather large circular driveway and on the other side of the Bycks was an abandoned golf course…our park, our football field, our baseball diamond, hide an seek, etc. etc…Donny Byck was my first friend and we played a lot.

I was 7 in 1939 when the German U-boats (submarines) started sinking ships in the Atlantic. We learned of the holocaust but had no idea what it really meant. We were in WWII and food and gasoline were rationed. Everyone did their patriotic duty in whatever way they could.

All along the Atlantic coast, towers were erected and 'spotters' like my Dad recorded all sightings of planes as well as ships...the US was on alert!...Dad used to take me along whenever he could because I was a good spotter for him...I knew every silhouette of every plane and ship.

My brother Hank enlisted and was made an officer because he had graduated from MIT...my cousin Morty Stern was in the invasion of Normandy as well as Africa and came back a bit shell-shocked...we now call it PTS... post traumatic stress.

I remember when I was 9 playing outside Ed Bry's house on West End Ave, when the Japanese bombed Pearl Harbor...We heard about the Japanese internment camps but didn't think much about it as we were on the east coast.

I soon realized that I was living two distinct lives. The first was during the winter with public school and kids living in small homes with modest incomes, and just enjoying 'playtime'. Having fun, with homework of course.

Then Memorial Day would come and all the families from New York and northern NJ would flock to the Jersey Shore. They would live in large mansions and drive fancy cars and have there own beach clubs and golf courses and they all loved my Mom and Dad.

Mom and Dad were made part of all the social events… they were invited to join the Ocean Beach Club, an exclusive club with a pool and ocean access…of course, to me it was just another pool where I knew everyone…I had such a good time as a child…I was a happy kid.

In the Summer, even the friends were different. My parents still had the Goldsmiths and the Brys and the Bycks and the weekly gin games but now I would see the Grads, Baerwalds, Murray Rosenberg, pres. of Miles Shoes, one of the biggest shoe companies, Phil Iselin, president of Monmouth Park Racing, Leonard Hess, owner of Hess Oil (future owner of the Jets), Leonard Block of Block Drugs, Arthur Garson of Lovable Bras, Sonny Werblin who founded MCA, (which became Universal Pictures) and the list goes on and on…and then Labor Day would come and the place was empty and I was back with the 'real' people and all the problems of normal living.

All my summer friends Johnny, Tommy, Ronny, Peter and Elson were gone…back to Lawrenceville Prep, Andover, Exeter, Petty and all the preps of that time and

I went to Asbury Park High…which I loved!…but that's another chapter!!

To sum it up…my childhood was a blast!…and we had no Little League, no surfing, no TV…OMG!!

Being Jewish

I guess the first time I realized I was Jewish was when I got on the school bus and was greeted by the local florist's fat son Peter Fabiano, "Hey Kike!"...I hadn't heard that word before so he repeated "Hey Hebe, why are you going to school on a Jewish holiday?"

...and I didn't know the answer.

Ros, my mom, just said that reformed Jews don't observe the second day of Yom Kippur and I should go to school...so I did!

I didn't know anything about religion because my Mom and Dad never went to synagogue and the subject never came up...until one day they said I should go to Sunday School at the synagogue to learn about our religion.

So, every Sun morning starting in October, I went to learn about the Jewish Faith. This went on till the beginning of the Christmas Season which now starts the day after Thanksgiving but in those days started the second week in December.

One of the first things the Rabbi told us about Christmas is that 'we don't celebrate it!' Jews do not celebrate Christmas: We celebrate Hanukkah. We do not sing Christmas carols and we don't have a Christmas tree!

I was in a bit of shock because we had always had a tree and I used to believe in Santa Claus!

When I got back home, Harry and Ros (Mom and Dad) asked about Sunday school? So I told them just what the rabbi said.

My Dad started to turn red with anger and finally exploded 'no rabbi is going to tell me not to have a tree and I will sing Christmas carols if I want to…AND we are going to have a tree…with lights!…and that is the last time you are going to Sunday school, period!'

And that was the extent of my religious training.

The subject never came up and all my parents friends just laughed and had a good time together. We ate at somebody's house every Sunday night and I frankly never heard any references to being or not being Jewish, although it was the 'Essen and Fressen".

In fact, I never knew what a bagel was until I was in high school and a new friend, Jay Kern asked me over for brunch and we had bagels, lox, and cream cheese... together!...a wow moment!

I was starting to get a sense of just what being Jewish was all about...at least the food part.

However, racism did not make a mark on me till I started to play high school sports

So, there I was, on a basketball team, the junior varsity and I was the starting guard and Jimmy Williams was at center. The other three were Remo Strada, Tony Annecharicco and Anthony Carrido...three whops, one hebe and a black (because I don't use the N-word).

The perfect formula for racism...the Italians don't like Jews or Blacks, the Blacks don't get along with the Italians and the Jew...well, need I say more?

Actually we all got along and laughed a lot at each other until the game started. Once an Italian got the ball, the Jew and the Black never saw it again...

And if the Jew or the Black got it first, the Italians might as well sit down and eat lunch!

The coach tried, as well as he could, but he didn't have a chance because, unbelievable as it may sound, we won…'racism is ok if you can laugh about it'…I think!

Anyway, if you are Jewish, you are going to encounter prejudice and racism, but you have to treat it like 'water off a duck's back' just find the humor in it or walk away.

Remember, you have to be taught to hate!…and the Jews I know didn't fit into that category.

When I went to college, there were two Jewish fraternities that 'rushed' me. One was Phi Epsilon Pi and the other Tau Epsilon Pi who immediately invited me to the SNDCFKK club but I had to pass a test in order to participate on a regular basis. The food was amazing: lox, whitefish, fresh Jewish rye bread, bagels, corn beef, pastrami…I know you are wondering…Sunday Night Delicatessen Club For Kosher Kiddies…and they had a test that any Jew could pass…I flunked!

I was such a 'bad' Jew. They had never met anyone with less knowledge of being Jewish than the kid from Jersey. I was the only Jew they had ever met that hadn't had a Bar Mitzvah (coming of age ceremony done at a synagogue).

There are three different religions within the Faith: Orthodox, Conservative and Reform. The Orthodox believe that they are the only true Jewish religion. The Conservative are slightly less religious and the Reform are the Liberals of Judaism.

The infamous test consisted of three questions: the first was to name three kinds of kosher salami…the second was 'How do you make a 'Necream' (Egg Cream)… and the third was 'What is a 2-cents Plain?'.

I never knew anyone that could pass this test!

I flunked the test but in case you are interested the three kosher salamis are Schmulke Bernstein, Issac Ellis and Hebrew National…a Necream is seltzer (soda) water with Nestle's chocolate syrup, and 2-cent Plain is just plain seltzer water. The bottom line is that I became a Phi Ep.

In college religion was one of the main topics for 'kidding someone'…I mean, my friends were all athletes and they were in Sigma Nu, a totally gentile fraternity, which meant no Jews.

All those Gorillas living together was 'kidding food" and I was one of the best...in fact they called me Timmy O'Stern, the Irish Jew and we laughed until we cried. I was brutally funny.

I encountered a different form of prejudice in the film business. When I entered the business, there was a great deal of bi-sexuality but it wasn't obvious because the guys were all married and the gay part was in 'the closet', so to speak.

So, in todays terms, I didn't know that Burt Lancaster was a bi-sexual until he asked me to run my lines with him and that he would help me since this was my first film. 'And about that Irish accent...I just don't think you need it!'

This was my first film, Hallelujah Trail and it was my first day and Burt was trying to help me.

I had been living in NYC and London and I sort of recognized the situation and politely thanked Burt, but I would just try and get through on my own but I appreciated his help.

David Rosen, my friend who was gay, always said that if a guy says he is bi-sexual, he really only likes guys.

After the film my agent, Joe Wizan, left William Morris and I went with Alan Ladd at CMA, another large agency. The first thing he sent me out on was 'The Pad' which was a famous play and was going to be produced by Ross Hunter, and directed by Brian Hutton.

I went to Universal and read for Brian who immediately took me to Ross to read it again. Ross seemed to be pleased and said to Brian, I guess we found our guy and Brian nodded to me as Ross said 'why don't you come over to the house tonight and we will go over your lines'.

The antennae sounded the alarm…

'Would love to Mr. Hunter, but tonight is not a good night', I replied. As I was walking out with Brian, he congratulated me on the reading and looked forward to working with me.

I felt pretty good about this when Alan called and sounded kind of strange. He wondered what had happened with Ross.

I said why?

Alan said that Ross had called and chewed him out for sending a rank 'amateur' to his office to read for the lead in his film.

I told him about the Director's comments and then it hit me…Ross Hunter was gay and had put the 'make' on me and was rebuffed…at least in his eyes.

Alan was very much a part of the game and things were never the same.

And that wasn't the only part I lost because I just wouldn't go that way. I loved women too much. I didn't care what a guy's or girls preferences were, I was just being me… I didn't smoke cigarettes, didn't drink and didn't go out with guys…period!

Germany offered me a glimpse into subliminal prejudice… "Oh, I don't hate Jews, I am not my father"… how do you go thru a war as the largest destroyer of Jews ever and somehow be totally cleansed. Perhaps it is buried deep and hopefully, will never rear its ugliness again.

I loved being a Jew in Germany. It made you aware of your surroundings and especially the history…two wars, one genocide, one dictator… I had one of the best times any soldier/guy could have … Jewish or not.

Family, humor, food, outlook on life are just some of the reasons I like being Jewish.

The Rooster

Every kid has certain events that happen while growing up that become what is known as 'teachable moments'.

In my case, I can recall several, but this is one that sticks out.

I was over at Donny Byck's house which was a large colonial mansion next to us and I was waiting for D in the hall by the stairs. The Bycks had a large house with a long hall which featured a large ornate mirror over a 19th century armoire. In front of the mirror was a golden rooster and it had a long history with the Byck family.

Since baseball was my passion, I was always practicing my swing in front of any mirror I might see and while I was waiting, I checked my stance and just waited for Donny. I saw a golf-club without the club part and realized that Maurice, the father, probably practiced his swing.

In any case, I picked up the golf-stick and started to swing it. Then I took it over and watched myself swing in the mirror…I checked my hands and where the 'bat' was over my shoulder and everything was good so I was ready to swing…imagining the ball coming I swung the bat and boom…tore the rooster's head right off and it landed on the armoire…holy shit!

I grabbed the head and put it back on the rooster and believe it or not, I hit it so square, that when I put it back, you couldn't tell I even hit it, there wasn't even a 'chip', so like any boy under these circumstances, I ran… back to my house…maybe they wont notice it!!

My mother came home and took one look at me and said 'what's the matter?'

I said 'nothing'…Ros said 'don't tell me nothing, when I can tell you are disturbed' now, what is going on?

I started to cry and blubber at the same time…'I was over at the Bycks and something happened!'

Yes…well…what happened…come on…spill it!…what happened?…now I was bawling and was totally incoherent…'I broke the roos…t..er'

You what?…b r o k e the w h a t?…stop crying and tell me!

I stopped crying and slowly said 'I was practicing my swing and I hit the rooster by mistake and tore the head clean off!'

The ROOSTER!!…My mother was in a state of shock… she couldn't talk!

I continued 'I tore it off clean, so I put it back on and you wouldn't even know I did it!

So, the Bycks wouldn't even know?…no chips?

I nodded twice.

And Donny or Maurice never saw you?

I shook my head no…

My mother thought about it for a moment…I thought maybe it would be ok.

Then she said…'Go tell Maurice'… face the music… go tell him!…now!

NOW, I pleaded…maybe he isn't home, I pleaded some more.

Ros pointed to the door…get going!

I left the house and slowly walked over, not knowing what I was going to say.

I walked in (nobody had locked doors in those days except at night) and called

'Maurice'…no answer.

'Maurice'…'Donny is not here', I heard Maurice shouting!

I want to talk to you sir…I said

Be right down…he said.

Maurice came down the stairs and said, hi Tom, what can I do for you?

I am so sorry Maurice but I have had an accident?

Are you alright?

I nodded. B u t...I broke the rooster!

He looked at the rooster and then back to me.

What do you mean, you broke the rooster?

I was swinging your golf stick and broke the head... of the rooster!!!

He went over and touched the head which MOVED...

It seemed like an hour passed in seconds..

GET OUT OF THIS HOUSE AND DON'T COME BACK...!!!

I left crying and cried all the way home, ran up to my room and cried some more...

Ros came up eventually to tell me that I had to tell my father the story.

Do I have to?

Yes!

Mom must have talked to Dad before he came up to my room because he said.

Sorry about your accident, but you said you were sorry to Maurice ...I nodded

Well, come down and have dinner, your mother and I will try to figure out what we should do, but I am proud of you for saying 'sorry'...that's not easy.

I was shook up but I slowly went downstairs and sat at our dining room table.

My Dad was a black/white kind of guy...no gray, and he lived his life like that.

GARAGE

You know, everybody gets in trouble when they are growing up!

When I was 10, Ronny Phillips and I tried quite successfully to burn down his garage...that is not quite correct.

All we did was to light a few quilts that were hanging on a line in the basement of a three-car garage...they were wet, we thought, so we knew they wouldn't catch fire, but they did!!

All I could do was ride my bike about a mile and a half home and cry big-time to my mom...incoherently, I might add. The fire-engines passed me on my way home...shit!

It wasn't my fault; all we did was light a few matches!... and all I could think of was what my Dad was going to do to me...oh, my God, was I in deep shit!

My Mom was a pussycat compared to my Dad...that's the way it's supposed to be...you know, good guy/bad guy!

So his punishment was for me to take my little ass, on my bike, back to the Phillip's house and take the consequences!

'Speak to Mr. Phillips and apologize and offer to pay for any damage and promise him that it will never happen again.'

And this is the worst part...Dad will not call Lloyd until I had handled it myself...OMG!

You know what its like to say you're sorry to anybody, much less a grown-up that's not your parent!

By this time it was night and the ride over seemed to take a long time...I was sweating bullets...

Thank God, Lloyd was great…he appreciated my owning up, patted me on the back and told me to go home!

'Teaching moments' are tough…but you have to go thru them…I guess.

Speaking of 'teachable moments', I remember saying to my Dad one day after Maurice Byck passed away 'you know Dad, Maurice was a nice guy!

My Dad said…'did you tell him?'

That profound thought has stuck with me my whole life…and I act on it whenever the occasion arises.

Monmouth Park

When I was fifteen I asked the owner of Monmouth Park Racetrack (who I knew from the Beach Club) for a job. He told me that I'd have to go thru channels and if it worked out maybe I could park cars in the lower lots.

In racetrack-ese that means the parking lots that were so far away you had to take a bus to get to the Track!

Anyway that's where I started and I didn't exactly park cars, I put my feet on a white line and allowed the cars to stop near my legs as I motioned the next car to the line.

I describe this because when you're making twenty-five dollars a week for six weeks, you start to invent ways to have fun and at the same time be remembered…so that, when they come out of the track and you open their doors for them, and pull out your trusty rag to wipe the dust from their dirty windshields, they would remember the nice kid that pretended to be a bullfighter on the way in and give him a quarter tip!...big deal you say...a quarter!!!

Well, consider this scenario...I made the dust when I parked the cars, so I guess six-hundred dollars in quarters ain't bad for a kid!

Ros and Harry were in a state of shock when I'd come in with my pockets full, and I can remember my Dad in hysterics as I showed him my toreador imitation.

I am sure you want to know if I bet or had any inside tips...every once in a while I would get a tip and get someone to place a bet but you have to remember, I wasn't a big horse guy...I never liked horses.

But...working there for three summers helped put me thru college as most of my college funds came from the track!

My last day was the best day.

I worked at the track for three years and the last day of each year was the biggest crowd, spending the most bucks.

By the third year I was in charge of one of the most prestigious lots at the track and I had many customers who would look for me because my lot was so close to the entrance.

I had about ten aisles of cars; each aisle consisted of a front row and another right behind with room to back up or go forward....

Except that on this day which was my very last day I decided to do something I'd always wanted to do...I parked all the aisles and then I parked all the rows as well thereby creating a total gridlock.

We all then went to a vantage point to drink beer and watch the chaos when all the people rushed out after the last race to get a head-start on the largest crowd of the year only to find that no one could move their car until the first car moved...who did this, where are the attendants!

Many beers were had that day amidst the laughter.... And they said it couldn't be done!

My Magic Bat

You know, when you were a kid playing baseball, there was always one bat that you wanted to use so, if a kid had on dirty underwear and used a certain bat and happened to go 3-4, you had better not be close to that kid, because he is not going to change his underwear until he has a bad game!…with that bat!…you see, all ballplayers are superstitious somehow and at one time or another, we have all had a 'magic bat'.

Believe me, the idea of a 'magic bat' never entered my mind as I came to high school weighing just over one-hundred pounds and being under five foot. I thought I would grow…but when?

Over the previous summer I was sent to a Camp Kennebec in Maine. So I got to play sports all day for a month. I played basketball and baseball and swam every day and I could eat as much as I wanted because the table I was assigned too had several guys that just were not that crazy for food so I was in 'food heaven'...ate everything in sight!

So, one of the councilor's (Mr. Rhinehart) taught basketball and much to my surprise, when I walked into the try-outs for Asbury Park freshman basketball, there he was...the coach.

I made the team and in fact, started the first game at guard (you have to understand something...when my dad put up the basket on our garage, it was the only basketball net in Oakhurst and so I was the first basketball player from Oakhurst and I had never played a full court game in my life) I was very nervous and didn't start again.

Made the freshman baseball team but I only hit .091... don't laugh!

In my senior year, I was 6ft tall...I punted for the football team, played guard on a basketball team that went to the state finals and hit .470 playing second base and led the state in hitting.

...and now for the 'Magic Bat'

As I was walking home from the bus stop, all bundled up as it was cold, a police car pulled along side me and stopped. The chief got out and said hi. I still felt a bit strange talking to the Chief of Police.

He said he was going thru a bunch of things in the barn, when he found this old bat and wondered if I might want it. I said sure and he said for me to just come over anytime on the weekend and he will get it. I said 'thanks Chief'

He said that he hopes its not too old as his door shut. It was Feb and burrrrr

That weekend I went over and we went out to the barn and he rummaged around and came back with the bat…it was huge…it looked to be a 36' inch, a beige ash with a rounded top…it was old but there was something strange about it…it was from another era. Of course I didn't know jack about the bat but I liked it. When I first swung it, it felt like I was swinging a log! Baseball was a month away so I just kept swinging it…I realized that it was so end-loaded that all I had to do was start it going…

The first few days of practice were just running and in-field with some light hitting. I didn't bring the bat. Then as we were nearing the first game, I brought it out. The coaches said it was too heavy for me and didn't want me to use it.

I said ok, just let me hit some batting practice and then I will use a lighter bat. As the coaches watched, I hit line-drive after line-drive…they couldn't believe it…but since it took me so long to grow, I had hit everything to the opposite field so I just waited for the ball and hit it to left.

And since I was a very good bunter and had good speed, it was tough to get me out and now I had another weapon.

This was a magical season…I couldn't miss and hit .470…it was nuts!

The bat came home with me every night. I polished the bat and talked to it…crazy!

The bat lasted for most of the season and then one sad day it broke…I kept the pieces for awhile and then I found a big heavy bat and kept on hitting, but…it was an other-worldly season with the Magic Bat!!

My Passion

Well, here I am in my 86th year on the planet and I am coaching 13yr olds in the Encinitas Junior League, playing on 90ft bases…they should be playing on 75ft like the 'Pony League' but they are doing it anyway.

I am an assistant, teaching some hitting and any other of the skills needed to make the kids better. What this means is that I have been involved with baseball for my entire life and I am still playing in two leagues and loving it!!

Ever since I can remember, baseball was the thing I most wanted to do. Oh, I loved many sports and played them all, but baseball has always had a hold on me!

It was the spring of 51' and I was on a baseball/basketball scholarship to the University of Connecticut and hitting pretty well when I developed this kind of fatigue that left me feeling kind of run down and always in need of sleep.

Finally went to the Doc who informed me that I had 'mononucleosis' known as 'mono' and that I had to go home and rest for more than a month which basically left me with a lost second-half of my first year in college.

In the late spring I was informed that the town I lived in (Oakhurst) was going to have a 'Pony-League' team and asked if I would be interested in coaching. I said yes immediately as I loved kids and actually thought I knew how to play and teach the game.

The year before I led the state in hitting and they thought I would be perfect for this team.

So, we had tryouts and most of the kids I had seen around and a big kid named Peter Grad came out. A kid who lived right behind me named Bruce Crowell came out as well.

I knew if I could teach them the correct 'form', I would have two really strong pitchers who could play other positions. Form was always my starting point for teaching.

Anyway, we had two weeks to prepare for the 'opener' and by that time, my team was ready.

The league managers got together and generally discussed their teams. The average age of the coaches was around 35-40 as they were dads helping out.

When they got around to asking the 'young kid' how he thought his team would do, I just quietly said that 'I didn't think we would lose a game!' That went over big!

We didn't lose a game for the first half of the season... I can teach baseball!

The league managers met again and discussed dropping out the 'black team' from Asbury Park because they 'just didn't seem to care about playing baseball'.

As they were about to vote on it, I raised my hand and said that as far as I was concerned, all kids wanted to play baseball!...it had to be something else...

The other coaches were dumbfounded 'so you think it's the coaching'...I said that I didn't know but I knew it wasn't the kids!...they were pissed!

'Why don't you coach them' smartass, if you feel that way?

I said ok, I will. So I gave my team to my assistant Don Byck, and I went down to meet with the parents and kids of the Asbury Park team. The parents knew me from seeing me coach the winning first-half team.

When I told them that the league wanted to drop the team because of bad attendance, they were kind of annoyed. I told them that I would coach them the second half on two conditions. I saw the kids looking at me…

The parents had to promise me two things. One, that the kids would make every practice and every game AND that they would be fed before each of the practices and games.

And if they did that, the Asbury Park team would probably not lose a game…they were in shock and the kids had never heard anyone say anything like that ever!

Asbury Park did not lose a game in the second half!

The finals were between both my teams and I coached the Oakhurst team to the championship and then picked from both teams to make up the All-Stars that played in the National Pony League Tournament.

We reached the regional final and the winner would go to Newburg, NY which is the equivalent of the Little League World Series in Williamsport, Pa. The kids were all together in barracks awaiting tomorrows game. The lights went out around 11pm.

The day of the game came and I knew something was wrong. The kids seemed listless and were not moving with any excitement…and this was the biggest game of their lives!

After a very sloppy infield drill prior to the game, I went up to Bruce Crowell and asked him what was going on?

He sheepishly told me that when the lights went out, Peter (Grad) said to Bruce but loud enough for everyone to hear, 'what did one coffin say to the other coffin?'

Darkness, quiet-time was broken with 'is that you coffin'!!

Laughter rang out and didn't stop for hours…the kids were hysterical!

We were beaten badly with Peter and Bruce making several errors BUT good times were had by ALL…

Dodgers

In the summer of '55, I was coaching American Legion because I had just come out of the hospital having gotten mono/hepatitis in college for the second time, and was doing my R and R (rest and rehabilitation) and had nothing to do, so I was asked to coach kids only a few years younger than me, but I had no problem with that. Apparently, they knew I had coached the Pony League a couple years ago.

When I came home one day, my parents were excited because I had gotten a letter from the Dodgers—the Brooklyn Dodgers! As I opened it, I had no idea what they wanted from me. I had hit well at UConn, but still. They invited me to a tryout at Ebbets Field in September, when the Dodgers were on the road.

There was no way I was going to be in any kind of shape but I thought 'what the hell' and replied that I would come. I used the coaching to get back some of the timing needed.

So, there I was, going to Ebbets Field in Brooklyn, not knowing how I would do, but determined to give it my all.

When I entered the stadium, I was shocked to see literally hundreds of guys who the Dodgers had invited just like me—the field was covered with guys. This was crazy; why did they invite me? How can they manage these many guys? Oh well, here I am.

Well, we all caught fly balls, we all fielded ground balls from short and then we were timed running to first base. Then it was box lunches for everyone. I looked around and more than half had been cut. Then the ones that were still there got to hit.

All through high school and college I batted left handed and only hit to left field, which was a bit unusual but I was fast and was a very good bunter. So when it was my turn to hit, I naturally stroked the ball to left field.

I hit okay but not nearly as good as I knew I could.

The Dodgers invited 350 guys and ended up picking only two guys to go to Vero Beach, the site of the Dodger spring training camp, and by some magical stroke of the wand, I was one of them, I was nowhere near the player I could be and still, they picked me.

New Years Eve 55'

It was New Years Eve in 1955 and frankly, I had just had a very rough year as I quit school because of hepatitis, which wasn't foolin around this time…it was a 50/50 life or death situation. And then friends of my parents, the Pollacks, delivered a half a cow to the hospital for me to get enough protein, the cure in those days for liver disease. The kitchen couldn't believe the amount of meat consumed by the kid on the fourth floor…me!

That year I had tried out at Ebbets Field, home of the Dodgers, was one of two chosen to go to spring training in 1956, changed my job location from Newark to NYC, thanks to a good interview with the David Marks Agency at 666 Fifth Avenue, gotten an apartment on Grove Street in the Village and since the Fall, had been living alone and having the time of my life.

Since New Years Eve was not one of my favorite nights, I was at home when the phone rang. It was Norman, a new friend from my favorite local hangout Louie's, who asked me what I was doing. I said "nothing", and Norman said he was coming over.

As we smoked a joint, Norman said he was taking me to a party and wasn't taking no for an answer. He said I would have fun, so, against my better judgment, I went with him. The party was given by a woman named Joyce, who I never met, as the place was jammed with drinkers and smokers (cigarettes).

Before you knew it, it was the bewitching hour and everyone started toasting the New Year and kissing everyone…it was 1956. I kissed a few ladies and turned to see this incredible brunette coming toward me…she put her arms around me and kissed me like I had never been kissed before…I didn't want the kiss to end but it finally did with the lady saying 'Happy New Year…I am Joyce and you must be Tom'…I nodded as that was all I could do, and as she left me smiling, I realized that this was gonna be a hell of a year…and it was!!

On New Years Day Norman called to say that we had been invited to a tea at Joyce's. I had never been invited to a 'tea' and although I knew I had no chance with a woman like Joyce, I agreed to go just to look at her.

About half way through the tea, Norman said he had to go and he split…after about five minutes Joyce said 'I suppose you would like to kiss me again?'

I kissed that woman for two months until I left for the Dodgers in Vero Beach. She was from England and had a child from a previous marriage. Just being with a woman of that class and style put me way ahead of the game at age 22…I was a confident lad!

Joyce was a woman not easily forgotten.

We have a Drink Together

Back in New Jersey, I got the official letter telling me that I was to report to Vero Beach in February, '56.

And in the following week I got invited by the Giants and the White Sox. They must have known all about the tryouts…and their spring-training camps were earlier than the Dodgers, so I decided to go to the White Sox training camp first, although I had no interest in them, but it would help me get in shape for the Dodger camp.

Actually I hit very well considering the time off, and was told that the White Sox would be interested in me except that I was Jewish and they made no bones about it…no Jews period. So I headed to Vero Beach as I didn't want to play for them anyway.

As I headed south, I realized that I had a few days before I was to report, so I thought I would see if I could go to Cuba, the gambling capital of the Caribbean.

I'd heard and read many good things about the Cubans and how beautiful the women were... but the island was a dictatorship run by a cruel despot named Battista and if you got in trouble you could kiss your ass goodbye...the notorious prison Guantanamo was filled with 'wise guys'...It was said that many went in but nobody came out.

I went to Miami and took a short flight to the island. It was only forty minutes away.

Cuba was just as beautiful as all the travel magazines said it would be...white sands, great food and extremely beautiful women that I could not communicate with, as I spoke not a word of Spanish.

Since I didn't gamble, I had to experience the two best things about Cuba...the palatial houses of ill-repute (the whore houses) and the rum factories. Both sounded good to me but of course I was twenty-three so anything sounded good to me.

The 'houses' were mansions set behind large gates. They looked like the estates of the very wealthy and had some rather large uniformed guards in front. They checked your identity and escorted you to the large doors at the entrance which swung open.

As I entered, I was met by a well-dressed attractive middle aged woman who greeted me in broken English and politely asked if she could be of service…I looked around to see a beautifully furnished living room with a marble staircase that went all the way up to the third floor. The woman clapped her hands.

The entire staircase railing filled up with women, one more spectacular than the next and the woman asked if I wished to be with one or more of them. I wanted to reply but I couldn't as my mouth was wide open with astonishment.

The next morning I sensed a sort of excitement in the city and I asked someone that spoke English what was going on. He said that a revolutionary named Castro was fighting his way out of the mountains and was hell bent on toppling the regime of Battista. He also told me to get out of Havana as soon as possible.

My plane was not till that evening, and I still had not gone to the rum factory. It was still early afternoon as I made my way to taste the rum at the Bacardi Distillery.

There I was, all alone, sitting at a table overlooking the square, sipping my daiquiri, thinking how fortunate I was to be able to see the real Cuba as it was a truly sensual city... so, I had another daiquiri and was just sort of dreaming...when all of a sudden, I saw soldiers running along the rooftops with their Neapolitan triangle hats with the white, crossed suspenders carrying rifles...there were literally hundreds to line the rooftops seemingly standing guard. For what I didn't know.

Then came the sound of motorcycles, many motorcycles that eventually weaved their way into the square. I had no idea what the hell was going on but I got a bit nervous seeing all this as I was alone in this distillery... and something big was happening!!

Into the square came more motorcycles, but this time, they escorted a very large limo. I was in shock as they pulled up to the distillery. The bartenders were all at the railing next to me...as the man got out of the limo, I heard them all say 'Battista' and they scurried around to make sure that everything was perfect.

First the guards looked over the room and... Battista entered, nodded to me and sat down at a table about ten feet from me.

So when anyone asks if while in Cuba, did I ever see Battista, I nod and say in my best Spanish accent 'We Have a Drink Together'!!

VERO BEACH

So, there I was in Vero Beach, home of the Dodgers. The Sandy Koufax, Don Drysdale, Pee Wee Reese and Roy Campanella Dodgers. Are you kidding me, these guys had been my heroes for years. I was a Dodger fan since I was eight. (I still am)

Vero Beach was full of ball players. At the time the Dodgers were the first to have all of their teams train at the same place. Major league, Minor league and free agents (the bottom feeders) all reported to Vero Beach. All told, there must have been 500 players there.

Two significant things happened to me in Vero Beach. The first occurred when Tommy Holmes, a former National League Batting Champ, approached me and told me that he thought I was a very good hitter but that my hitting to left all the time would not get me very far.

He said 'kid, on this next pitch, I want you to hit it with your left hip!' Knowing who he was, I did what I was told. The next pitch came and I swung just like he said and the ball left my bat like a rocket and bounced off the wall in right center. I was in awe. This had never happened before and I immediately became a 'power hitter'. In one sentence, he changed the way I hit a baseball…a wow moment!

Every morning I went and picked a grapefruit from the many fruit trees that lined the various fields. On this morning as I picked a big one and started to peel it, I noticed a group of executives walking toward me. Of course I immediately recognized the owner of the Dodgers, Walter O'Malley, among them. As they approached I heard Mr. O'Malley say "Hey Tom, how you doing?"

I was in shock. I answered in the affirmative 'Good, Mr. O'Malley'. He nodded as he passed.

How the hell did he know my name? I was one of the 'bottom feeders', one of maybe 50 free agents and one of 500 guys here. That was an unbelievable moment. A moment I would never forget.

I played pretty well down there until, while running out a double, I pulled a hamstring and the Dodgers sent me home.

The following week I got a notice 'Uncle Sam wants you'...I was drafted into the US Army!...it was the Korean War and they needed me.

You're in the Army Now!

It couldn't have come at a more inopportune moment as my Dad was getting worse and they were about to put him into the hospital plus I'd gotten the love of my life...at the moment...pregnant which was the first time that had happened, so all in all, I was having a bad hair week!

Being twenty-two at the time, I honestly thought I would beat this thing because twenty-four was the limit, so I figured I'd make the best of it and have as much fun as possible.

So, there I was at Ft. Dix, N.J. which is located about an hour out of New York in New Jersey. I reported to Red Bank, a town at the shore and we were bused up to the base.

It seemed that I was slightly older than most of the other recruits...but then, I was twenty-two and most of these guys were younger than that. Ft. Dix was both a relocation center as well as a basic training center.

The very first thing I learned in the Army was that there is no such thing as Logic...If you wanted to get along in the Army you had to think and act in the most illogical way so you would be locked into the Army's thinking!

Now, how did I arrive at that conclusion?...Most of the recruits sent to Ft. Dix for relocation end up at Ft. Ord, California!...That is where I was going to take Basic Training even though Basic Training was the primary function of Ft. Dix.

This will not do...my Dad is not well and they want me to go to California...I don't think so.

This became my first initiation into the "If you don't ask for it, you don't get it school".

I found an officer and told him, that I didn't think my Dad would live another year and that he was in Lennox Hill Hospital and I didn't really want to go to Ft. Ord sir!...if possible...

He looked at me for about a minute and reluctantly said that if my story was correct, and they would have the Red Cross check it, they would keep me at Ft. Dix for Basic Training...which they did.

The Relocation Center outfits you, gives you one hellacious haircut, your uniforms and generally harasses you for about a week until one night, just when you are having the best dream of your life, the one where you are about to kiss some beautiful creature … Bam!… the lights come on and the room is filled with Drill Sergeants. They are all hollering and throwing your covers off and screaming that you aren't worth living and that you should go back to your mother's womb, and of course its 3AM and your about to be shot because you are the scum of the earth and have leprosy.

You grab your gear and go outside, where buses await you to take you to the nearest concentration camp known as boot camp because that's exactly what you're going to get up your ass and probably tonight.

The bus finally stops and loudspeakers in human form scream at you to run with your 80 lbs of gear to somewhere where you stand at attention while the Top Sargent who is black, 6'4 and 300 lbs tells you that your body no longer belongs to you, your mind no longer belongs to you and that if you wish to breathe any longer… you must ask his permission!

He then introduces you to God, who is a piece of starch, black, with bars on his shoulders, who is carrying a big red book containing all the laws governing your next two years of your miserable life in the Army...and since he goes strictly by-the-book, their is no need for thinking...blah blah blah blah blah...we may now sleep for an hour before the bugle sounds...no problem!!

Dad is in rough shape, I want to see him as much as possible and right at this moment I decided to go for it... put it all on red...I was not of sound mind or body. At my first opportunity which was right after the morning slop, I head straight for the Top's office...I fire a salute and request permission to see the Captain.

The Top looks at me like I'm totally out of my mind and says...Why?

I said it's a personal matter sir!

Top said...what's the personal matter about?

I said it's a personal matter sir!

He said...look asshole, nobody sees the Captain unless I say so ...so what is this personal matter about soldier?

Its none of your fuckin' business... sir!

Dead silence!

Top is about to become totally unglued and kill me with his bare hands...I mean, this is the first day of basic training and some little piece-of-shit is about to...

The Captain roars...GET THAT MAN IN HERE, TOP!

So there I am, in front of the starch, go by-the-book, black Captain and after I salute, he says...what's the problem soldier?

I say 'I'd like every week-end off sir'!!!

The first sound I hear is the stifled laugh of the Top as he practically falls off his chair...nobody, but nobody could have the balls to ask that, unless he was trying to get out on a section eight, which in the big red book means that you are crazy and the Army would then throw you out.

The Captain 'Oh, you want every week-end off...the sarcasm oozed out...and Pray Tell, why do you want every week-end off, if I may ask?

After taking a deep breath, I said that my Dad was dying, (which I had learned he was) and I'd like to see him as much as possible...sir!

Well, you could have heard a pin drop in that office, as the Captain stared at me for what seemed like as eternity and finally, he said 'private, if this is true...you got every week-end off!'

I said thank you sir and fired off a crisp salute and left.
I got a pass every week- end during basic training much to the consternation of everyone that didn't know.

Never Volunteer

Within Ft. Dix, there were 12 to 15 regiments, each made up of around 1000 men and each regiment thought they were the best, so there were always competitions going on...I remember the Top asking for volunteers to compete in tennis and swimming.

I'll be damned if I was going to volunteer...you never know if he is tricking you or not...I'd actually gotten friendly with him and he shook his head in disbelief every time he saw me, but I liked him...and this was on the level...they actually were going to let guys out every afternoon to practice.

My first question was where were they going to practice...the tennis courts were about one minute from the company, but the swimming was at the base pool...sort of like a country club...so, I guess I'll go for swimming; so what are the events...400 yard freestyle, the 400yard backstroke, the 400 yard butterfly, and the 400 yard conventional breaststroke.

Although I did all the strokes, there was no possible way I could even finish 16 laps of the pool...so I signed up for the conventional breaststroke...you know, the one where you pretend to be pushing away the garbage...hey, I knew I couldn't win, but I could finish!

So every afternoon I went to practice my suntan...oh, I mean swimming...what a life...by the way, I neglected to tell you that if you won for the dear old regiment, you got a weekend pass.

The meet came and it was crowded...there were 10 guys in my race...the gun sounded and we were off... when I casually reached the 10th lap, I looked around and I wondered what in the hell was wrong...there was no one else in the pool...had they all beaten me?...no, I guess there was a great deal of garbage in the pool, because I was the only one to finish...

Ft. Dix conventional breaststroke champion...hero to my regiment and the recipient of a three-day pass, which I already had, but I felt good about it...it sort of took the pressure off the captain.

I was then invited to represent Ft. Dix in the east coast Army Championships that were being held at Ft. Monmouth which was about 3 miles from my house...aw gee, I'd have to keep practicing for another two weeks...

out of the eight week-ends in basic training, I won four of them and was given the others.

I should have realized how unreal this Army experience was going to be when our company went to the rifle range...they were going to pick a group to represent the regiment in the base rifle competition...anyway we lay down to fire and I must tell you that I had trouble seeing the target.

So when I heard somebody say in a deep southern accent "Oh my gawd, will you take a gander at this", I knew that somebody had shot the shit out of the target and it surely wasn't me.

Then I heard someone say "Hey boy, where did you learn to shoot?"

I started to reload, when I heard this voice say Stern, the Major is talking to you!...I jerked my head around... me?

The Major had his glasses up to his eyes when he commanded me to fire another six rounds which I did...the Major said "we got one here...and he handed me the glasses and sure enough, the rounds were all grouped the size of a quarter...you could have knocked me over with a feather.

They gave me another week-end and I represented the regiment and won my event.

At the end of basic the captain called me the best non- soldier he had ever known and the Top loved me as well...I was told that I was to be trained as a clerk typist and I was staying at Dix.

So, I started as a clerk typist till they heard I'd been down with the Dodgers, they asked if I'd like to play for Ft. Dix...

I naturally said no, I couldn't...yeah, right! I was going to practice baseball every afternoon away from my company...oh, I couldn't possibly.

I played about five games till they realized I was getting no training at all, so they sent me back to my company.

Oh well, it was good while it lasted.

Korea or Germany

The Korean War was going on and it was an ugly war for a very different reason...the North Korean Army had more soldiers than bullets, so they would send massive amounts of troops at the US troops until we ran out of ammo and then they would overrun the positions causing us to constantly retreat and regroup...this meant a long drawn out and many-lives-lost kind of war...the kind I didn't want to attend!

My Dad was about to fade, so I was a bit crazy...and one day I went and found the Lieutenant in charge of the destiny of my clerk-typist company. I was very surprised to find an attractive lady officer asking me what I wanted.

I replied that I'd already learned in basic, that if I didn't ask for something, the chances were that I wouldn't get it, so I...ah...ah...ah wanted to express my desire to serve the Army in Europe...if possible!

The sarcasm oozed from the Lt.

Oh, you mean you don't want to go to Korea.

How strange, she replied, you mean you don't want to shoot a gook?

I was dead meat...I might as well pack my Asian undies cause I had just fucked up!

I blurted out, look, I meant no disrespect, I would just rather be in Europe than in Korea so I thought I'd ask. I snapped off a salute and dwarfed out.

Don't ask me how the zone works but needless to say I was the only one in my company sent to Europe!!!...go figure!

I said my goodbyes and hugged my Dad an told him I loved him.

We headed to Germany and were routed thru Prestwick, Scotland for some strange reason, stopping for fuel at an airbase in a small town outside of Glasgow.

The town was famous for one thing...it was the birthplace of Robbie Burns, the poet, and his castle was known for its scotch whiskey. I headed for the castle because I heard it served 20 year old scotch and besides, I had never seen countryside like that before.

As I was waiting for the bus, I noticed everyone staring at me, so when I got on the bus, I asked the driver what was going on?

With a thick Scottish brogue, he replied that no one had ever seen an American before and the chances are that there would be a party that night for all the Americans at the center.

The twenty-year old scotch was everything it was supposed to be as I staggered back to town to find a party like no party I'd ever seen...you see, all the eligible males in the town were in the British Army, so there were ten women to every guy and they were ready to party...and we did!

Needless to say a planeload of very hung-over privates headed for Frankfurt, Germany to begin their European tour of duty.

Frankfurt

None of us knew where we were going, but when I saw Frankfurt, I knew I wanted to stay there.

I took a walk around and suddenly found myself looking at what looked like a stadium sticking out surrounded by ruins. I went in and was shocked to see a beautiful baseball field just sitting there and I wondered how in the world a field like this was just sitting amongst the bombed out ruins and I realized that NACOM (northern area command) must have had a General that was a 'sports nut' but whatever the reason was, I knew I had to stay here…r u kidding me…a ball field in Frankfurt…heaven!

I loved being in the city but I had a feeling I was headed to the border, which was on 24 hour alert because of the Russians. I got my orders and sure enough, I was headed for Schweinfurt, the 'pig city', on the border…no thanks!

I headed straight for Special Services where I pleaded to see the colonel.

He's not here, but the Lieutenant will speak to you.

Sir, I really don't want to go to Schweinfurt.

The Lt. smiled 'you don't want to go to the beautiful pig-city of Schweinfurt?

The man has a sense of humor.

Look Lieutenant, I played college basketball, I was down with the Dodgers and kicked field-goals in high school which was a lie. I'd say anything to stay in Frankfurt.

He was the baseball coach which was cool but he told me that I would have to go to the pig-city and they would ask for me in order to try out for the NACOM basketball team...but I had to go!

The next day we went on maneuvers and three days later I was given orders to rush home to New York as my father was dying.

I arrived too late. But he and I had said our 'good-byes' before I left. He knew he was 'leaving the planet' and we had already expressed our love for each other...

my Dad was a great man. I stayed a few days to be with my mother and then headed back to Frankfurt.

When I got my new orders, I was staying in Frankfurt...thank you Lieutenant...I was back in the zone!

Well, basketball practice started and frankly I didn't know if I could make the team, but as soon as I heard how the jocks were treated, my whole game went up a notch!

You see, if you made the team, you lived with the team, ate at a special mess and had no hours...no reveille, no curfew, no commanding officer to bust your balls and get this...no uniforms!

This is my kind of Army!!!!!

The General was the jock of all jocks, an egocentric fantasy Hall of Famer, a unanimous All-American in his own mind, the Heisman Trophy winner, MVP candidate and...you had better win baby!

I mean, this was a tough life in Frankfurt...you slept as late as you wanted, ate as much as you wanted and generally had the time of your life...but, you practiced till you dropped!... but who cared.

I started at guard and we won...the General loved us.

Game On!

Every weekend we got a pass and every weekend we knew we were going to get one, so the problem became, where to go?

I decided that I would invent a game that even I wouldn't know the destination!

On my pass I would list all the countries that I could get to and back by Monday dawn; Lets see, I could go to Paris, Brussels, Copenhagen, Amsterdam, Munich, Hamburg, Geneva, Nice etc.

So, I put all the countries on my pass and went to the Hauptbanoff (the Frankfurt RR Station) and the deal was that I had to take the first train out to wherever it went as long as it was on my pass!!

What a wonderful game this was...My first trip was to Munich during Oktoberfest...the only thing I can remember was dancing on a table with the other two-thousand people, drinking huge steins of the best beer I can remember and eating chicken like Henry Vlll till I couldn't move and at the height of all this, I looked over and this beautiful girl was laughing at me, I thought, so I went over and she became one of my wonderful memories of Munchen!

For the next year or so I had no idea I was in the Army...every weekend we didn't play, I went to the station, played 'the blind travel game', and away I went.

Christmas in Germany was like a funeral...no parties, no celebration, no nothing...So I found myself on Christmas morn, walking on the docks of Amsterdam which wasn't exactly joyous either.

But it was beautiful, a new experience and as you can tell, I loved the nervous anxiety associated with something new! A stranger in a strange town...Losing my identity has always intrigued me.

Anyway, I was walking along and a couple with a child passed by and I wished them a Merry Christmas and they said the same to me as I went on.

About five minutes later I felt this tap on my shoulder and it was the couple I had passed. I was surprised when they asked me if I was an American. I said yes and they asked me if I had a place to go for Christmas dinner. They said I looked like I was alone and although they were not very well-to-do they would feel privileged to share their meal with me.

Christmas makes you very vulnerable and I was alone and what the hell. I said thank you very much, not having any idea what I was getting into.

They were poor and our dinner consisted of cheese, bread, some wine and a little fruit, nuts and coffee. He was Jewish and had hidden in a cellar for four years…her cellar…she was not Jewish.

He was a graphologist: he read handwriting for corporations; that is to say, when an executive applied for a job, he would be required to write answers to certain questions and the handwriting would be analyzed as to his qualifications and the corporation would hire this way.

It was one of the most interesting Christmas I have ever spent.

Another time I was in Paris visiting Bernie Davis, an old friend of my folks…the most unusual man I knew at the time. His son and I were good friends but I thoroughly enjoyed listening to the stories of all the places that Bernie had been… Bernie had been everywhere many times...he told me once that he had been around the world fourteen times!

(NOTE to J and N: remember our trip to Kyushu... Bernie looked and had the same body language as the Shinto Priest...small, joyful and moved like a duck...very, very knowledgeable about a great many things.)

Bernie treated me like a friend and so when he suggested that I meet him in Paris, I knew it would be memorable. In Paris no one eats until at least 10pm so Bernie thought I'd like to go hear this blues singer before dinner. She was beautiful and had a wonderful sound. She also took off her clothes...she was so sexy I could hardly stand it!! Bernie could see I was enthralled, so he embarrassed me completely by asking her over after she was finished.

Well, if you think I was embarrassed when she sat down, try to picture my expression when she was introduced as a man! She was the top female impersonator in Paris and I swear I didn't see anything resembling a man when she, I mean he, was nude...Bernie did it again!!

This Private stayed at the George V on the Champs Elysee and ate at some four-star restaurants with the infamous Mr. Davis...the city was a dichotomy in that it was so beautiful and yet so unfriendly! You see, the dollar was worth so much more than the franc, that Paris was besieged by Americans...rich Americans...need I say more.

In those days the average American had never travelled except in a war, but then again the French didn't like anybody anyway.

Paris was a challenge to someone that didn't speak French. I definitely wanted to go back there.

I had been told that there was one city I should avoid... Brussels...it was cold, unfriendly and the women were like the weather...cloudy and overcast...not a pretty picture!

Well, wouldn't you know it, the first train out was going to Brussels and I never second guess myself...first train out...I had to be on it!... and I was...and they were right... Brussels was cold, unfriendly and the girls looked like the weather!...

However, there was a square in the middle of Brussels called the Grand Place that appeared to be lit in gold. You could sit up in a tower, drink hot wine and think you were back in the Renaissance.

It had to be one of the most romantic places I'd ever seen...if I had a girl...which I didn't! And there was no Bernie...I didn't speak French and when I asked anybody if they did, I got the standard "no compre misseur".

There is one type of female that might speak English... that is one that is in a uniform and I saw one walking in front of me, and if I timed it right, maybe I could just come up to her at a light...how clever the over-amped, testosterone-oozing-out male can be!

This is it...she stops as the suave, debonair American comes up next to her...he pauses and then says "Do you speak English?"

She looks at him like he was dog-manure and replies, as the light turns green "Of course...I'm American!".

He catches up to her because this beauty is not "cloudy and overcast" and tells her that he is here from Germany, alone and would love to take someone to have a glass of wine at the Grand Place?

The direct approach: it was the only one I knew...and it worked...so there I was drinking wine with a beautiful older woman who was married and just passing thru...she was a stewardess and her husband was a steward for Pan Am...

Men do not make decisions regarding sex... if she wants to, you will...well, after several hot wines, she asked me whether I had ever smoked Hashish and when I replied no, a smile came across her face and in that moment I knew that whenever anyone tells me not to go somewhere, I'm going!!!

Baseball in Germany

Although I was only twenty-four years old, I had a feeling that this was to be my last year of competitive baseball. Somehow I couldn't picture myself making it to the majors before age twenty-eight, so as far as I was concerned this was it!

And there was only one position I had never played... pitcher, so I went out as a pitcher and the coach actually thought I was a good one...I will confess to anyone that I had absolutely nothing on the ball except my hand...but as a hitter, I could spot a weakness and I could exploit it...in fact, I started the first game and won with a three-hitter. I also had four hits batting in the customary ninth slot.

The Lieutenant (the coach) came up to me and told me that he knew I wasn't a pitcher after seeing me hit, so where did I want to play. I said first base, so the next game I batted 5th and played 1st base.

The General had never seen me play, as the first game was an away-game, but since he had built this great ballpark in the middle of Frankfurt, the man never missed a game.

The field was the best one in all of Europe and the foul lines were about 340 down the lines and 420 to right-center and 450 to dead center.

Joe Hicks was already signed to the White-Sox and he could do it all, so in the first game at home, when the score was 6-4 against us in the ninth, two outs and men at second and third, they walked Joe to get to me...

The General was going ballistic as they brought in some lefty with a great fast ball who was signed with the Yankees.

As he warmed up, I looked back at the General and I couldn't help but laugh to myself at the circumstance. I'm in the Army and it feels like college and the General is a serious fanatic!...so, on the first pitch, I hit it out, over the 420ft. sign and Frankfurt was mine...I became the King of Frankfurt!

I was in the zone!!!

To give you some idea of how insane the Army really is, the General gave me his car whenever I wanted it and the use of his apartment in Frankfurt...he would have made me a member of the officer's club, if he could have....that summer was like a dream and I was floating thru...

I had a season to end all seasons. I led Europe in hitting, home-runs, doubles and I was second to Joe in runs-batted-in and in women taken home after everyone else had to go back to the base because of curfew!!! Two scoundrels in Frankfurt!!!

NOTE: Oh yeah, I forgot, I was made a Private First-Class which lasted until the MP's caught me in the back of an ambulance celebrating my promotion.

PFC for half a day and a night for a new Army record!!!

The Dilemma

Since this was my second year playing basketball, I knew I'd make the team, so I was very relaxed and as a result played better...

Winter was approaching and one night a group of young Germans approached me and asked if I would come to watch them play basketball and maybe talk to them.

I said sure and as they left, it dawned on me that they didn't know I was Jewish, and if they did, would it matter? Being in the heartland of Germany, I made it a point not to get myself involved in the obvious.

Anyway, I went and watched them annihilate the other team, so they were very happy as we went for some wurst and beer...

As they settled in, they begged me to critique their play and I told them that although they beat the other team handily, they lacked some of the basics such as 'defensive rebounding, outlet passes and an offense that moved the ball faster and recognized the open man, just a few things needed to compete at a higher level.

They were very gracious and I saw no need to bring up any other issues at that time...they had a girls team as well, so there were about twenty in their club.

After our next game they were back again and this time they invited me to their club dinner, and maybe talk some basketball to the whole club...so to be nice, I accepted.

The next night they picked me up and we went to a restaurant and down in the cellar was a banquet room filled with about seventy kids, all members of this club. I was placed at the end of the table as the guest of honor.

It was weird and quite honestly I thought I was back in 1939 at a Hitler Youth meeting, but that was my own paranoia.

After dinner, the President, who was sitting at the other end of the table, stood up and spoke about the future plans for the club and how they aspired to win the German championship in their division and after much cheering, he said that in order to do that, they needed to take their game up a notch and so this meeting was called to formally ask me to coach them!!

The cheering started and they began to bang the table and chant "We want Tom".

I was floored...I didn't know what to do, I told them that maybe they should ask another German, because if I coached, they would lose most of their games this year!

A bit of a murmur was heard.

"You must understand that in order to go forward, you will have to go back and start all over again in learning the basics, in other words, you would be taking a step backward in order to go forward!! Do you want to do that?"

A thunderous yes!...I didn't answer right away as my mind was working overtime on the Fabiano issue...the Germans hate Jews...right?...maybe not!

Everything seems to be in slow-motion as I contemplate my next sentence...
"Do you know that I am Jewish?"

"Of course", they reply, "but we are not our parents, we are the new Germany!!"

So I coached them. As I had predicted they lost most of their games that year. The following year, however, they won the German National Championship in the B division…as I told them they would.

I was happy for them all the while never forgetting that there were many Sterns killed during the war. Some buried in the main cemetery above Frankfurt while others never given a proper burial at all.

The Shit Hits the Fan

We were about to start baseball season when the impossible happened...NATO, which was made up of all the allied forces changed their policy and the General was ordered out of Frankfurt...OMG!!!

The day he left, all the athletes were ordered back to their companies..

You will wear a uniform, you will stand all formations and you will not receive any special treatment...is that clear!!!"

These words resounded throughout Frankfurt and presto, we were back in the Army...horrors!...I had about ninety days to go, when I reported to my commanding officer whom, up to this point, I had never met!

In fact, I had to find my uniform as I hadn't had it on in more than 17mo...now that is disgraceful!!!

Have you ever seen a dog waiting for a steak: Well there was Captain O'Connor, the saliva coming out the corners of his mouth and steam foaming around his nose as he gleefully awaited...my arrival!!!

After I came in and saluted him, he read me the riot act.

I handed him my orders which were in a sealed envelop and were considered classified information. He opens the envelop and proceeds to turn beet red and with smoke coming from his nostrils he bellowed...

"Private, there is no way in hell that the U.S. Army is going to pay you for unused leave time"

I'm thinking 'What the fuck is he talking about???'

I looked at him in total disbelief, because I had already used the sixty days leave time I was entitled to, plus all the time on passes

So I was in total shock when he said...

'With all your special service time, you neglected to take your leave time...this means that the Army would have to pay you close to $1000 on discharge!!

...NO FUCKIN WAY!!!...

A hint of a sly smile crossed his tight-lipped mouth... he had me and he knew it...I had a hammer bangin away in my stomach...

When an officer smiles at you, the shit is about to hit the fan!!! He drew a big breath and bellowed...

"Soldier, you are ordered to take 60 days of leave effective 1200hrs today and I do not want to see your sorry ass around here period or it will be mine!!! Do you understand? "

Yes Sir I shouted!!!...I could hardly contain myself as I snapped off a salute...one of my friends had erased my leave records and my punishment was a 60 day vacation... oh, the searing pain...help!...somebody get me off this torture rack...what can I do?

Springtime in Europe

Its springtime in Europe and it's been grey and cold in Germany, so you know where I was headed...south, but there was one problem...cash!...

You see, you need cash to get around Europe and a Private was hardly in a position to travel for sixty days with no cash, so I collected all the gas stamps I could from everyone and got on a train headed for Rimini, on the Adriatic coast...looking for sun...and maybe a black-market in US gas coupons.

As absurd as it might sound, my final destination was the Brussels World Fair which was something I'd always wanted to see, and it was happening in 58'.

But I also wanted to see Rome, Capri, and a bullfight in Spain...so anyway, it was warm in Rimini, but there was no interest in my stamps, but since you cant get a bad meal in Italy, I was feelin' good!!

I knew I had enough to get to Capri, so when I got tired of the beach I headed for Rome...by train with all the families and all there belongings including some chickens and other animals.

While in Rome I wanted to see the Vatican, the Coliseum and the beach...most people don't know that about thirty minutes from Rome is a beach and and coming from Jersey, I always want to go to the beach.

Anyway, I walked around a corner of Saint Peters square to see the Vatican and frankly, I was overwhelmed with the stark beauty of the Vatican and immediately knew why the Catholic Church was as powerful as it is.

St. Peters square was awesome, beautiful, but scary and that's the way the church ruled...thru fear.

Eating in Italy is fantastic and that is even if you only eat pasta and wine.

Met a G.I. who knew a guy who knew a guy that might buy all my stamps.

Were they any good?...sure they were good...they were perfect...he looked at me with a jaundiced eye as he paid me the money, and I knew in that moment that it was arrivedirchi Roma!!!!

A train between Rome and Napoli is something to be experienced...when you went to Naples, you took everything with you...kids, dogs, farm animals, grandparents and you name it...by the time we were out of Rome, I was offered food, wine in exchange for news about New York and Chicago and considering the fact that I spoke no Italian, this was hysterical...I mean everyone was drunk and laughing...who cared what I spoke...it was great!

There was a Naval Air Force Base just outside of Naples and naturally I checked to see if I could hitch a ride...they said sure, if I was going to their destination and there was room...

So after checking out Pompeii and stuffing myself with seafood and pasta of course, I took a ferry to Capri for the good life only to find that the island was almost entirely gay...Even though it was not my scene, I had a great time people-watching Went back to Naples and the Navy...they had a plane and room to...Frankfurt...no thanks.

I have several weeks to go...tomorrow a plane is going to Madrid...matadors, flamenco, guitars and the bulls...I'm on it...

Of course the bullfights are sold out and have been for months...

Now the only thing to compare to the Army is a bell-captain at a major hotel, so logic dictates that you march up to the chief ball-busting, bell captain at the best hotel and simply ask for a ticket to the bullfights and after he laughs till he falls down...you might score...

So, I head for the best hotel in Madrid, The Ritz and sure enough, there was a very large captain ordering everyone around...I walked up to him and asked for a ticket and he laughed in my face...but he didn't fall down and I thought I might be in trouble...I needed a new approach, so when the laughter subsided, I handed him a twenty-dollar bill and asked again...he looked at the twenty like I had just insulted him and reached under the desk and handed me a ticket...gracious senor!...ole!

The reason most people say they like the bullfights is that it's sooooo artistic, but the real reason is, that after several margaritas and/or beer in the sun, they frankly don't give a shit my dear!!...bulls, what bulls...ole! The bulls didn't do much for me, but the people-watching was sensational.

Now for the fun part...I was running out of cash and I had to make the Worlds Fair in Brussels somehow...the Navy doesn't fly that way, you know what I mean?...so, its hitchhiking or a train...hitching thru the Pyrenees with the Basques hating the Spaniards somehow did not appeal to my military cowardice, so its the train thru Paris overnight to Belgium...

When I arrive at the Fair, I have just enough dinero to get in, see all the sights, eat and say hello to my friend that works there, and finally, get a taxi to where else, but the U.S. Consulate! I'd heard that when a G.I. turned himself in the consulate made sure he got back to his base!!! Wrong!

The Last Hurrah

Can you imagine the look on the Captain's face when he got the call from the Consul General in Brussels demanding to know why one of his men had the audacity to demand his return to his company because he had no money...and just what was the Consulate supposed to do with him???

Although I know he put his hand over the mouthpiece and shouted at the top of his voice "Fuck em where he breathes"...

He said "The private will reimburse all expenses...I'll personally see to it, sir!

"You will paint this entire building before you leave this Army". And if you mess up just once, I'll find a way to extend your time...do I make myself clear?

I had two weeks to go...would I make it?

I had a cyst on my hand and the Army has to fix everything before discharge, so after painting for one day, I pulled out an appointment slip I had and the next morning I went to have the cyst removed...no biggie...

Except I got real friendly with the Doctor, who was also getting out in a week, and asked him for a sling as an excuse for not painting the building...

The Doc said 'You must be joking; no one in your condition can possibly do that kind of manual labor for at least 10 days...

Thanks Doc!

That will leave me 3 days before going home...I can't wait to give the Doctor's orders to the Captain, who is going to have a myocardial-infarction (heart-attack) on the spot!!...and he does!!!

With about three days to go before giving up the sling con, I hear the scuttlebutt that when I go back to the relocation center, prior to shipping out by boat, they were going to get me...they were going to find something to hold me...anything would do!

As I was thanking the Doc for his help, I couldn't help but tell him that I had learned in the Army to ask for what you wanted, because if you didn't, the chances are you aren't going to get it!

The Doc looked at me 'What do you want now?'

Well, I hate boats and besides, somebody has it in for me...so what are the chances...

Needless to say the Doc sent me home by plane and as a matter of fact, the day I was supposed to report to the relocation center, I was heading for the airport and home...

The luckiest soldier to EVER be in the Army...is HOME!

Back from the zone

Most guys would opt for a vacation before trying to get back into the workforce, but because I had been on vacation for the last two years, I wanted to start earning a living and more importantly, I wanted to find out if I had any talent for acting!!

After all, I loved being in front of people and hearing them cheer so why wouldn't I see if I was good enough to earn a living doing something I love to do...what a concept!

So, anyway, I interviewed for a position with the David Marks Agency.
I liked the idea of working on Fifth Ave and 53rd St. because it would take me ten minutes to get to the office and New York City was such a visually exciting place to be!

I had always liked the Sheridan Square section of the Village so I found an apt. on Cornelius St, near the one and only, Louie's, the one place that I could lead a a double life…Insurance salesman by day and hippie by night.

The Life Insurance business afforded me the luxury of time…I mean that it wasn't a nine to five job. I was able to meet enough people by joining the Harmony Club and the Hollywood Golf Club at the shore…I played squash during the week all year around and golf/tennis on the weekends, when I visited my Mom.

As you both know, I love anything with a racket or a ball, so I became enamored with squash to the point that I started at the very bottom of the ladder and won the club championship my first year, and held it for two more years thereafter…not so with golf, where I was known for the longest throw of a golf club in Hollywood's history! I was forever losing clubs in trees and lakes, where most of my drives landed!

Now add in my classes at the Stella Adler School of Drama and imagine the girl-crazy lunatic that is now your father or your grandfather, or your great grandfather and you have all the ingredients of my lifestyle in 1959-60.

You probably don't know much about Stella, but she used to be part of the Stanislavski school, which became the Actor's Studio. Brando, Montgomery Clift and most of young leading men of that period came to Stella...the rumor was that she slept with some of her students!

Stella liked me because I always came to class in a nice tailored suit but I was a bit shocked when she came up to me one day and asked what I did for a living...so I told her I sold life insurance and she then asked if I would mind coming over to her apartment to look at her policies?

...look at her policies...are you kidding me...policies?? Was this a come-on or what? I mean, Stella was a terrific, but she was 60 years old...there's no way I was gonna ...her policies?...and yet, how could I say no to Stella Adler...I couldn't!

So, there I was, going up to Stella's apt on Fifth Ave., at 5 o'clock one afternoon...I knocked and a uniformed maid answered the door. I told her my name and she said that Ms. Adler was expecting me and that I should go right up to her bedroom!

Bedroom!...your kidding me!...no way jose!...shit, what the fuck am I supposed to do...I thought of various negative answers to the obvious..." Gee Stella, I'd love too, but my gonorrhea hasn't cleared up yet!" or " Stella, I wasn't planning to admit this to you, but I'm gay!"

I reluctantly entered her bedroom to find Stella...in bed no less!

...and you can imagine my surprise and relief, when I saw about twenty insurance policies spread all over the quilt!...I took out my handkerchief, and wiped away the sweat that had broken out on my way to her bedroom.

Stella's studio was located on 39th St. between Park and Lexington and I would go there at least twice a week for two years.

One day during my second year at Stella's, I was doing a scene from "Rose Tattoo" and in the middle of the scene, I forgot my lines.

The reason I remember the moment was that I can remember the stillness, not a sound, and I realized that the audience was waiting for me to continue...I had them! In that suspended moment, I knew I could be an actor!

Rain

One day toward the end of the first year, a significant event occurred...it was raining 'cats and dogs' when I got out of class and naturally, I had an umbrella.

I went to the corner of Park Ave. and 39th St...it was impossible to find a cab...it was just as difficult for the beautiful blond next to me!

I asked her if she would like to wait under my umbrella and she answered "au, oui, masseur!"

She was gorgeous, a model and French ...I was finished, on the spot!

I finally found a cab and we got in... she knew no English and I no French, but I had to see her again... somehow!

I don't know how we managed, but we met for coffee and I was smitten...I thought I could learn some French and Claudie thought she could learn English...she won!...but I didn't care...and guess what...

Claudie lived on 39th St.... Heaven!...I had died and gone to heaven.

Classes became the highlight of the day...we were together for two years... sort of...

We lived together in the village and uptown at 67th and Madison...we couldn't live with each other and we couldn't live without each other...it was never dull.

I remember taking Claudie to the Beach Club...it was the first time anyone had seen, much less worn, a bikini to the club.

My poor Mother...Ros took more flak on my account, but...she loved the controversy, until one week-end while visiting her, we had a fight, and Claudie locked herself in the bathroom...

I used to have a bad temper, and I ended up kicking in the bathroom door... That was the last straw...

Ros threw us out of the house!

Claudie taught me how useless jealousy is and we finally broke up when I told her that I was going to be an actor...

She left New York for California and I have never seen her since...but Claudie was something else!

A Close Call

In 59' I was approached by Billy Roberts at the Harmony Club. He asked me if I was open to an opportunity to make a bunch of money in a short period of time.

After thinking for a nano-second, I nodded and he said...

All I would have to do is go to Connecticut weekly to keep an eye out and report back to him on the day to day activities of Marvin Botwick, the President of Consolidated Research and Development Company, which was traded over the counter as a penny stock. The company had several patented inventions that were being marketed.

Billy and friends had put up the start-up monies and had controlling interest in this company currently traded at $.06 a share. For doing this for him, his group would give me a salary plus 200,000 shares of restricted stock which would become tradable in a year.

The thought of going into show-biz with some money was very intriguing as I didn't want to become a waiter or do some other menial job in order to survive the rigors of showbiz.

So, I accepted the deal and headed for New Haven to meet the president, Marvin Botwick and Sal Cuomo, the Executive Vice President. Marvin was very nice and showed me around the company and introduced me to the various products they were marketing.

One product could fix your flat tire and blow it up at the same time. Another product could be installed in your engine and would make your ordinary brakes 'power brakes', capable of stopping 'on a dime!' Both were patented and both were awaiting a marketing entity to start the ball rolling.

After coming to New Haven every week, Marvin began to trust me and one day, he took me to a back room to show me something he was working on that was a 'top secret' in his world…he took a piece of glass and applied a solution to it and asked me to breathe on it…nothing…no condensation formed…this solution would be applied to glass and would stop any condensation from forming…imagine, a windshield that was always clear… no more having to wipe the windshield when you entered the car or truck in the wintery or rainy morning…

(remember, this was before defrosting and heated blowers in the cars/trucks)

Perhaps the biggest use was to increase the efficiency of a power-plant by reducing the condensation on the pipes in the plant…a mind-boggling invention of gigantic proportions and an investment bonanza for the stockholders of this little company.

When I told Billy the various uses of this material, he said that he would come to New Haven the next day and to arrange for Marvin to be there.

When I told Marvin, he told Sal to get his investors here tomorrow as well.

So, although I was not there, I was told that Marvin put on quite a show, everyone was totally impressed and Billy said that he was going to try to get Ford or Chevrolet interested…

The stock started a meteoric rise in value going from .06 to $1.00 to $5.00 to $10.00.

All on rumor of interest from the car giants.

You can just imagine what was going on in my brain… I was going to be rich!

The obvious sale of this 'coating' was to the car companies and between Marvin and Billy, they got Ford and then Chevrolet interested. The stock went to $15.

One day Marvin told me they had a presentation arranged at Ford and then at Chevrolet. And he wanted me to go with him…Sal would be there as well.

This meeting information got leaked and the stock went thru the roof, rising to $20. As the time approached, the company was in a frenzy preparing for the presentations in Detroit. The stock kept rising going to $25.

Billy Roberts became my best friend, calling twice a day wanting all the latest developments as the day approached. Ford had booked a hotel in Detroit and you could cut the excitement with a knife…everyone was a bit nuts at the possibilities. The stock went to $30…that's 6M to me if…

So, Marvin, Sal and myself headed to Detroit for the presentation and I am told to stay in touch with Billy, day or night, as the stock is now $32.

We arrive at the Hotel to find that Marvin has been given the Presidential Suite…everyone is excited, as we all go down to the bar for a drink.

Its 4AM and I am wide awake with this sinking feeling in my gut…I personally had not seen the patent pending, or any paperwork nor had I even seen the formula for the product or the ingredients…and I was going nuts!.

Of course I knew that Billy and the other investors had probably seen everything but I am nervous because I have been put on the Board of Directors and the stock is going thru the roof. If anything goes wrong, it could be a major, major problem…like going to jail!

I go up to Presidential Suite and knock loudly because I know he sleeps deeply and is difficult to wake. I knock again, several times and finally the door slowly opens as Marvin appears with his eyes half closed and asks "what the hell are you doing waking me up?"

I say Marvin, I am so sorry to wake you…its just that I am very nervous…I know this is stupid and I am positive that you and Billy have gone thru all of this but would you mind showing me the formula or the patent-pending on this solution…

Marvin says, "go back to sleep, I got this covered!"

Show it to me please!

Marvin wipes his eyes, coughs and says 'there isn't any formula. I just know how to do it and it has always worked'

I am in a state of shock!...my mind is shouting in my ear...no patent pending, no formula to see, and he is saying 'I got this covered'...my mind races!

I have never felt so bad in my life...I am definitely going to jail!!!

I say quietly 'You mean, we are going to the Ford Motor Company and when your stuff works, you are not able to show them a formula?

Marvin nods...but I have it all under control, I can deliver the formula!

My head is just shaking back and forth in astonishment...

Marvin, 'I am not going to jail for you or anybody else, I am calling Billy this instant!'

Marvin says 'go back to your room and relax, don't get Billy in an uproar over nothing'

I went back to the room and immediately called Billy, awakening him...he said, 'what the hell are you doing, waking me at 6 o'clock in the morning'.

'Have you seen the patent pending or the formula for the 'coating'?

And he replied 'no, I have not seen anything'…I thought the attorneys were covering that!

THERE ISN'T ANY FORMULA!

So I told him the story and he was appalled…the very first thing he said was 'if we don't blow up the company this instant, we will all go to jail'

So he did…He notified Marvin to cancel the presentation and an announcement went to the financial press as well as to the various markets well before the 9:30AM opening.

Trading in the stock was halted…the stock was suspended…everyone lost everything.

I never knew who Sal Cuomo was, but I later learned he represented the investment of the 'guys from Rhode Island' and they were pissed! When my name was brought up as a 'problem' that should be 'taken care of', Sal told them that I had done the right thing and after some discussion, they agreed…reluctantly.

There were no charges by the SEC and I went back to the showbiz path…this all happened in six months.

My First Job

Toward the end of the two years with Stella, I wanted to expand my talent, so I enrolled in an 'improv' class run by Wynn Handman. I loved improvisational acting and while in Win's class, I got the idea of 'commercials' and thought that commercials would be something I could do.

So, I found a commercial agent who sent me out on my very first interview. It was for a 'Handy Andy' commercial.

In those days, everything was personal…no tape interviews like today…anyway, I read the copy with the casting lady that called me in.

Every commercial had a 'punch line' at the end to help sell the product and when I said 'Can I give you a helping hand lady' to the casting lady, she blushed and cleared her throat.

The account exec said the reading was to sexual and dismissed me.

The next day I got a call from the casting lady who asked if I smoked and I replied 'of course' knowing full well that I didn't and wouldn't...but I would for a commercial!

She asked me to come in that afternoon to J. Walter Thompson who at that time was the No.1 ad agency in the world!

I immediately asked my assistant to come in and then asked her to smoke.

She said, why?

I told her about the commercial possibility and she lit up and I lit up.

She held the cigarette a certain way and I imitated her.

She put the cigarette to her mouth a certain way and I did it exactly the same way.

She inhaled and I inhaled and promptly coughed my ass off...there is no way I can do this, this way!

So, she did it again and I did it again BUT I inhaled like I would a joint…slowly and I didn't cough…OK, I am ready!

As I entered the agency, I was in a gray, double-breasted suit and I looked good.

I was ushered into a room full of account-execs all dressed in Brooks Brothers suits with button- down shirts with four-in-hand knots in their ties all holding what appeared to be Ticonderoga pencils and yellow pads on their knees…the uniform of the day!

Everyone including the casting lady seemed to be in a good mood as they asked me to sit down and have a cigarette.

There was only one place for me to sit…an easy chair with a table next to it with a jar of Chesterfields and small jar filled with wooden matches.

I sat down, crossed my legs, took a Chesterfield from the jar, a match from the little jar and lit up and put the match in the ashtray…

Took a long drag and as I exhaled I noticed that no one was watching me! The 'suits' all left there seats and were tamping the Persian carpet…my match had missed the ashtray and had fallen on the very expensive carpet.

When they got back to there seats, no one wanted to admit that they hadn't seen me smoke so they asked me if I knew how to fish off a beach.

Well, I was brought up at the Jersey shore near Asbury Park and of course I fished with my father many times, so the answer is 'yes'!

Anyway, I became the 'Chesterfield' man...smoking badly right-handed and casting left-handed which drew over 500 letters asking if they turned the film around because I smoked right-handed...so, I did three more and my pic turned up in Life Magazine which is: **THE COVER OF THE BOOK**

I've never smoked...cigarettes!

The Chesterfield commercial opened many doors and I did seven or eight more and that led to my signing with (my first and only New York Agent), the late great Monty Silver!

But He is George to Me!

The very next week I went for an interview with Monty Silver, a one-man, small theatrical-only agency. I liked him and I guess he saw something because he started to send me to several auditions for parts he told me up front that I would never get! But they would give experience!

So I was in Actor's Studio taking a class with Lee Strasberg, when Monty called and said I had an audition for the Florida run of yet another play I wasn't going to get, a comedy to be directed by the infamous Mr. Abbott called "Never to Late". It was to be an open call, so I could go at any time.

Monty thought it would be a good idea for me to see the play first, so I went to see it that night. Orson Bean, Margaret Sullivan and Phil Ford were the stars.

It was embarrassing how hard I laughed at this play. It was so funny that I had to go back the next night. The audition was the following day. It was just as funny the next night as I stood in the back and howled!

When I went to the audition, the stage manager gave me the play to read and said that when I was ready, he would get me in for the audition! I looked around at the fifty guys all reading, and I said to the stage mgr. I'm ready!

His look said "what do you mean you're ready?" I repeated that I was ready and he said "Okay, let's go!" He wanted to add smartass, but he was the assistant stage mgr.

He took me right to the lit stage and gave me the two audition scenes. He introduced me to Judy Abbott and two other men who were there. I knew the scenes they were auditioning, because I had practically fallen out of my seat laughing at them. I read the scenes perfectly! It didn't feel like I was even reading them, I was so comfortable with them.

Judy Abbott complimented me on the reading and asked what experience I had. I smiled and replied that I didn't have any!

She actually laughed at what she perceived as a joke! She asked again and emphasized that it didn't matter how small the roles were, just be frank and tell her and the two producers some of my credits.

I said that I was sorry, but I didn't have any!

They were floored and I was excused. Since Monty had told me that there was no chance I was going to land this part, I was loose!

When I opened the door to my apartment, the phone was ringing! It was Monty; What the hell did you say to those people?

I replied, I didn't say anything, I read and told them that I had no experience! Why? What's the matter?

Monty said, well, you gave the best reading of the day and they think you're lying, they want you to read again tomorrow!"

I said Monty, I know this part, this is my kind of humor! I'm going to read the same way... what should I do?

Monty said, I don't know, just tell them the truth, you're not going to get it anyway! I thanked him for getting me the audition, it was fun!

The next day I read again, the same way, and again Judy asked me to tell the truth, so I did, and this time the Producers were aggravated, they wanted to know my story!

So I told them that I'd been at Stella Adler for two years, I had no experience on stage, but that I was used to performing in front of crowds, because of sports, and that I felt an affinity for this role! They said thank you and I went home.

Two days later, I was called back and I noticed the assistant stage manager treated me well and there was only one other guy to read, Tony Roberts! Tony Roberts, just one of the best actors in NY!

I read the same way and left.

The next day Monty called. He said that he had just received a call from Judy Abbott. It seems that she was casting the show, but her father, Mr. Abbott was going to direct it and that she wanted me for the role, but the producers wanted experience.

She called Monty to let me know that Mr. Abbott, as he was called by everyone and I mean everyone including his daughter, had called the producers and flatly stated that if they wouldn't accept Tom Stern, then he would bow out directing the show!

I was blown away, you gotta love the guy!

Well, I got the show, and went into rehearsal in New York with Fred Clark and Joan Bennett in the starring roles and Monty negotiated an "Also Starring " billing for me!...Not to shabby for a guy with no prior experience.

We would head for the Coconut Grove Playhouse in Miami, two weeks before we opened, and Mr. Abbott would take over! Fred and Joan were petrified of meeting Mr. Abbott. He was a tough old guy that ruled the Broadway musical comedy stage and was a total icon. You name it, he's done it!

Having been brought up in Jersey, I had always gotten along with the older men at the clubs I belonged too. They had experience and were easier for me to talk to than the younger guys my own age. And I used to kid them a lot and they loved it!

So when I met Mr. Abbott, I liked him immediately and although he was tough, he was fair, and sometimes even listened! And he had a great sense of humor, he kidded Fred unmercifully and Joan too!

The night of the opening, everyone was a nervous wreck, but me. I don't know, I felt like the first day of baseball season! The opening was very exiting and it went well, I got good reviews!

Ros and David Rosen came down from N.Y. and they really enjoyed it as you can imagine.

The Producers, who didn't even come down, sent me a telegram wishing me the best. Of course I got it the next day and they misspelled my name! They hated me, but other than that, everything was good!

Mr. Abbott was a golf nut, so when he found out that I played, he invited me to play with him and it was always enjoyable. He told me that this show was the out-of-town run for a London engagement, but that the Producers wanted to recast some of the parts.

He was referring to mine of course, but I went along with the flow, causing no waves. But I did call Monty as soon as I got home and he told me in no uncertain terms that I was not going to London.

The other notable event was the night that stage-fright caught up with me. I've always been late with emotional response, so two weeks into the run I forgot my lines, not some of them, all of them! I was a wreck and had to be prompted the whole show!

Well, I came back to N.Y. and went to Troy, N.Y. to do the Yum-Yum Tree with Margaret O'Brien who was a big star then.

This run was notable for two things. The first was that Ms. O'Brien was allergic to water! She refused to take a bath and my love scenes with her were torture! I had been sentenced to olfactory hell for two whole weeks!

The second thing I'll will never forget was a performance, where during the first act, the power went off and I improvised with a candle, actually it was funny and the audience laughed at the problem. Then I noticed during the first curtain call, dust coming down from the ceiling. As I looked up, I saw the pipe that holds the curtain, start to tear, so I pushed everyone back, as the pipe came crashing down on stage!...a hero is born...saved about three people that night.

Arrived back in N.Y. to find that the argument was not resolved re: The London Company of Never To Late. I called Judy up and she said that Mr. Abbott was about ready to leave the Production, that he and the Producers were fighting about my part. The Producers wanted to cast an English actor as it would be cheaper!

Well…Mr. Abbott did it again…he gave another ultimatum and one day Monty called to tell me that I was going to London! We were going to play the Prince of Wales Theatre in Piccadilly, the heart of the London theatre area, a 1200 seat musical-comedy theatre.

I loved London and London loved me! Our personalities were perfectly suited for one another. Those were the days when the English ladies known as "birds" loved Americans.

Bare in mind, I was paid six times what the English actor would be paid! I made 145 pounds a week($300-400). I lived in a mews house in Ebury Mews, Belgravia, and paid 80 pounds a month with a maid!...I lived very well, thank you!

Being an American in the theatre gave me carte banche to all the private clubs in London. They even invited me to the RAC, the Royal Athletic Club! Actually, I was probably the only Jew in that club! Anyway, you get the picture!

The rehearsal went well and we were getting ready to take the play to Oxford, Manchester and Birmingham. I started to play golf with Mr. Abbott on a rather regular basis and I looked forward to playing these incredibly beautiful golf courses as we traveled...what a tough life!

After playing all the courses in Oxford, we headed for Manchester and on one occasion, while playing on the 13 hole, I said to Mr. Abbott as we were about to tee off "Mr. Abbott, how about a small wager?"

He smiled…

He asked 'what do you have in mind?

I said 'I want to bet your first name'

Mr. Abbott looked at me and a smile broke out on his face and he said okay!

He won the next hole, but I won the next three and when we approached the 18th tee, I said "George, hit away!"

He started to laugh so hard, he had trouble even hitting the ball and then he laughed all the way down the fairway.

He told me that I was the only person in the world that had his permission to call him George, and that I also had his permission to tell the story!

The next day, at rehearsal, Fred Clark, Joan Bennett and myself, were in the middle of a scene, when Mr. Abbott interrupted and gave me a slight change.

I said George, do you think I could do it this way?

As I was about to show him I looked and everyone was frozen! No one had ever heard anyone call this icon George!

Fred Clark marched over to me and chastised me " How dare you call him by his first name?" He is to be called Mr. Abbott!

I turned to Fred "He may be Mr. Abbott to you, but he's George to me!"

The White Elephant

There is no way to describe what London was like in the early sixties except it was the epitome of sex, drugs and rock an roll! My suits, shirts, shoes, ties were all made to order. I wished the show would go on and on, I was having a great time!

The Americans had a baseball game every Sunday at Hyde Park, across from the Queen's stables. The English were known for their foot/eye coordination, but they couldn't throw a ball across a room! They would come to see these crazy Americans play 'rounders' as they called it.

You know it's funny, everywhere I've ever gone to play any kind of sport, I'm looked at like I can't play anything! If I go to play tennis, someone has to volley with me to be sure.

So, when I asked if I could play, the big guy in charge, threw a few with me and saw that I could catch and so, he put me in the game and when it was my turn to finally hit, there were two men on base. On the first pitch, I hit a ball over the 500 year-old oak trees that line Hyde Park Rd., the street itself, and the oak trees on the other side of the road! The ball went over the wall of the Queen's stable, never to be seen again!

To this day, whenever I meet anyone who was in London during that time, this hit is remembered!

Each night when the show was over I would go and eat dinner at any one of a half a dozen of the best eateries in London and I knew the head waiters by their first names and they knew me! My favorite was a place called the White Elephant!

One night I was eating dinner when I spotted this redhead who looked like no one I'd had ever laid eyes on and she was with a guy from the States that I knew…I couldn't believe how beautiful this girl was, so I wandered over and said hi to my friend Kenny, thinking he would introduce me, but he wouldn't!

The son-of-a-bitch let me stand there! Finally, I left and returned to my table, but I was pissed! I vowed that the next time I saw this incredible girl, I would establish a new world record in "hovering" until whoever she was with introduced us!

A week went by and frankly, I was getting tired of eating at the same place.

Then one night she came in with an agent that I had met by the name of Dennis Selinger. So, when they had finished their first course I excused myself from the group I was having dinner with, and went over.

I said hello to Dennis and after what seemed like twenty minutes, but was probably more like five, I introduced myself, "Hi, I'm Tom Stern!" and Dennis was too embarrassed not to say anything, so he said "oh, I'm sorry, this is Samantha Eggar!" I shook her hand and looked into those green-gray eyes and that was the end of me!

I went back to my table and told everyone there, that I was going to marry that girl! They looked at me like I had just had a lobotomy "You're going to marry Samantha Eggar huh? You'll be lucky if she even talks to you!"

I figured that if she would meet me for a cup of coffee, I had a chance!

She wouldn't meet me, period!

Then after many calls, she agreed to meet me before my show for a bite, but she wouldn't come to the show… She wasn't fond of the American Theatre!

I guess she had never met anyone like me, because she agreed to see me again... and again etc.

We were now an item, but she refused to acknowledge the relationship...she had been in love with Albert Finney and that had broken off, but it still lingered.

Sam got "The Collector" and was going to film in London directed by William Wyler...she was going to star in the film with Terrance Stamp...she was happy!

We were living together and having a great time.

Road to Hollywood

I landed an episode of "Espionage" using pure chutzpah! I convinced the Director that he didn't have to get an actor from Hollywood because I was already in London!

It only took two interviews, a telegram and a late night phone call that woke the poor man up.

The Director finally gave up and later told me that my persistence got me the job.

I shot the show in the daytime and did the play at night…fun

The show finally closed and the T.V. show was to be shown first in London then N.Y.C. the next week and finally Hollywood the following week.

Sam and I talked and decided that I should go follow the TV show as it was the only film I had and maybe I could get someone to see it! Meanwhile, Sam was going into rehearsals and would have no free time anyway, so that was that!

I followed the show to New York where I saw Ros and my friends, and immediately headed to Hollywood to find an agent, if possible.

In those days Monty had no affiliation in Hollywood, so I was on my own.

I was staying with a friend of a friend and was there about a week, when I got the name of an agent at William Morris, Joe Wizan. I called and told him how I followed the Espionage segment to the coast and was looking for an agent and would he see me?

He said he would and I went to the William Morris Agency, the most powerful agency in Hollywood and was told that Joe Wizan was the 'up and coming' star of the agency. His assistant, Barry Diller, came and escorted me to his office.

Joe talked to me for about five minutes before picking up the phone and making a call. "I found the Irish teamster, when can we come over?" He put his hand over the phone and said to me "Can you do an Irish accent?" I gave him my best Barry Fitzgerald and he laughed. Okay, we'll be there tomorrow.

My very first meeting in Hollywood was with John Sturges, one of the most famous Directors of that period...he directed the Seven Samurai with Steve McQueen and many other classics such as "Bad Day at Black Rock": with Spencer Tracy etc.

Joe introduced me and I said 'howcha do sur' in my best brogue and Sturges said that I looked like McQueen. He turned to Joe and told him to call business affairs!

I had no idea what he was talking about until Joe congratulated me "You got the part!"

He then told me it was the biggest picture of the year! "Hallelullah Trail" was to star Burt Lancaster and Lee Remick and it was going to cost a staggering amount of money...7 Million Dollars! My part O'Flarety, was the head of the Irish Teamsters!

So, I got an agent, a three picture deal and an "also starring" credit on my first picture...all in 10 seconds.

Well, back in London Mr. Wyler woke up with a cold and didn't feel particularly 'chipper' one day, so he suggested that they move the 'shooting' to Hollywood, where it is warm and comfy...imagine moving an entire film company because the director has a cold...it could only happen in 64' and it did!

So, Sam was on her way over here to film and we were going to live together...not a bad week. The studio found her a house off of Sunset Plaza...

Sam was a fabulous lady, but single-minded when she worked. Since she was in practically every shot, she was called at 5:30 am every day, and was coached every night by Kathleen Freeman, before going to bed at 9.

We saw each other briefly and usually on Sunday, but a problem arose when I wanted to go out. She wanted me to stay home, and for me, that was impossible.

You really find out about actors when they work and she was difficult at best. I'm 32, just got a role in the biggest film of the year and I am in Hollywood for the first time...not good for a monogamous, stay-at-home relationship!

On weekends we were invited everywhere...we were on the A-list! That meant we were on the beach with Roddy McDowell, tennis at Jack Hansons and screenings at Mel Brooks etc etc...Samantha was in a very important film, she was a star!

When Sam's picture finished she decided to go back to London, she wasn't comfortable with the A-list social life that we had gotten into.

I was loving it and while I waited for my picture to start, I decided to see other people and one morning I woke up and realized how much I missed her and called her and asked her to marry me! Actually I was a bit shocked when she said yes!

Hallelujah Trail

The first shot of my film career in Hollywood is worth recounting. I arrived on the set in Gallup, N.M. and was told to see the director. Sturges welcomed me and said, 'one of the assistants will take you down to the train, you'll be in the tenth wagon and when the train passes this spot, the crane will swing down right next to you and you'll start your scene with Brian Keith. You'll then hop off the wagon and we'll cut, you got that?' I said yes because I had no intention of saying 'What did you say?'

The assistant drove me to the wagon train some two miles away. My wagon was the tenth in line. I was driving four horses.

NOTE: They sent me to learn how to drive horses and on the first day the so-called expert wrangler was showing me how to hold the reins, the horses went out of control and he ended up yelling for me to jump and then pushing me off before the crash!

So, to begin with, I wasn't exactly comfortable with the horses. When the first AD said to move out, it was like an echo. Move out!, move out!... It must have been repeated ten times, all the way down the line.

We finally started to move and the camera was nowhere in sight. We went for more than a mile and out of the corner of my eye I spotted the crane with the camera, high up and to my left. We kept going and the camera was finally coming down toward me at a very slow rate. It kept coming and coming until it was right next to me in a tight close-up!

I was far too guilty to even think of messing up my lines. Imagine having to reset the entire wagon train again because Tom Stern forgot his lines! Anyway, as I said my lines, the director said "Cut it!" Holy shit, what did I do wrong?

Sturges said "It's not your fault Tom, it was a camera problem, let's do it again!" P.S. It took an hour to reset the shot.

Burt Lancaster tried to give me a lot of fatherly advice until I picked up the fact that he was bisexual! Lee Remick was stunning and Martin Landau, playing an Indian with blue eyes was hysterical. Donald Pleasence was the consummate actor!

Meanwhile, Sam wanted to be married by a certain priest in the Westminster Cathedral! Did you hear what I just said...WESTMINSTER CATHEDRAL...are you kidding me...Tom Stern kneeling in the WC ! Anyway, all she wanted to know was when I was going to finish, which I thought was reasonable for a marriage.

So, I called my agent who called the production company. And they gave us a date that we could plan around. I then added a week for "Murphy's Law" (everything that can go wrong...will) and we arrived at a date of October 17th. Sam booked" Westminster Cathedral" and the invitations went out. David Rosen was my best man and Paul Baerwald and Peter Grad would be in the wedding party with my brother Hank.

As the date approached, I could tell that I wasn't finishing and I realized that they didn't know that I was getting married! I called my agent who called the production company. My agent told me to postpone the wedding as the company was running over! I said "go fuck yourself, I'm getting married!"

That's the first time I heard the word "unprofessional." I told him that he better tell the production company that on the 15th I'm leaving the set! Well, everyone went crazy and when it was over, Sam had to cancel the wedding! We understood, after all, we were in showbiz.

So, I said to my agent, when can I get married? He called the powers that be and they said that they would definitely be finished with me the following week and we could set a date one week later. Sam had to move the wedding from Westminster Cathedral to St. Johns, a beautiful little church in the Belgravia section of London. Thank God! Can you picture me getting married in Westminster Cathedral, I don't think so! Anyway, it was set!

Right! It was set until the next week when they asked me to cancel the wedding again! You know I have a temper, and have been known to blow it! This was one of those times, especially when I heard the phrase "unprofessional."

Take your "unprofessional" and stick it up your ass!

Anyway, they finally agreed to let me go on one condition, that I return the following Monday, they had to shoot me on Monday! Had to!

It took all I could muster not to shout out 'bullshit'…I didn't believe a word they said.

Ahead of My Time

After the wedding and the film we moved to Hollywood, where I found this amazing house on Cielo Drive in Beverly Hills where Nicolas was conceived. We were there for six months.

We tried to buy the house and were shocked at the price of $110,000.

This turned out to be the house where the 'Manson Murders' took place several months later.

After our arrival in Hollywood, I met a few people and started to play softball for 'The Daisy' which was a club owned by Jack Hanson.

When he learned that I loved playing tennis he invited us to his mansion on Beverly Drive, where we met Stan Cantor and other athletes as Jack was a total star-gazer.

Stan invited me to play doubles with him at various courts and we became friends. When we weren't playing, we talked about the 'biz' which eventually resulted in us forming a company called 'Tracom Productions ' (tragedy/comedy).

We opened an office in Beverly Hills and put our name on the door. I was ready to get involved in 'Production'.

We pooled some money and as a first endeavor, we were the first company to get the rights to 'Logan's Run'. Of course, no one thought that this 'futuristic' book would ever be made into a film. We were turned down everywhere because no one was even slightly interested in reading a 'book'.

We also were able to get the rights to 'They Shoot Horses Don't They?' Again, we were unable to get any interest. We wanted to make a small indie film in Santa Monica. It was a 'dance-a-thon' and was truly a literary masterpiece, but still no interest.

This 'book' was only sixty-five pages and still, no one would read it!

Since I had been in 'Never To Late' and Norman Lear and Bud Yorkin were making the film, I got to meet them and were told that my part was going to be played by Timothy Hutton.

But I got along well with them both and eventually we (Stan, myself, Norman and Bud) tried to get the rights to 'The Natural' because we all loved baseball and this was the ultimate baseball film of that time. We got close but 'no bananas'!!

It was during this time that I happened to run into Stanley Schneider, the President of Columbia Pictures, who invited me to his office. When I got there I showed him several comics and he asked me why I showed him comic-books?

I said 'those comics are not comic books Stanley, they are story-boards' and you, my friend, are going to make every one of them…mark my words!

Well, we couldn't hold the rights to any of these projects and they were ALL made into hit films…Logan's Run became a hit at MGM, Sidney Pollack made 'Horses' and Robert Redford starred in the Natural…and all the comics were made into films!

So, I guess you might say that we were 'ahead of our time'.

It was at that point that I lost contact with Stan and frankly, I cant even explain why. He went on to Produce films and I went on to do the biker films.

Lets see…I made the first biker film (Hells Angels 69) that got an M rating with the original Hells Angels.

After our divorce I moved into the house on Horn and began the Clay Pigeon odyssey which became the first independent 'Vietnam' film. Only the studio 'Green Berets' with Lee Marvin was made before mine.

Several years later I found 'Victory' which was the first soccer film anyone had even thought of.

I had gotten Warner Bros interested because they owned the 'New York Cosmos' with Pele. They offered me a 'development deal' for low low dollars but it was a 'studio deal' which I had never had…I turned it down. (mistake)

It was eventually made by Freddie Fields who gave me a Co-Producer credit but I neglected to contract the placement of the credit…so, on your way out the door after seeing the film, if you happen to turn to see the last credit on the screen before it goes 'black', you might see my credit but I doubt it…(another mistake)

Well, I found Victory in 72' and it was made in 82'…so I guess you could say I was 'ahead of my time'…so what!

I made the first big-wave surfing film with Columbia in 35mm…up to that time all surfing was shot in 16mm but I wanted to do a feature on 'big wave surfing' in the 90s.

The guy that green-lighted the film was fired as we were in production so I knew that the film would not have the backing necessary for the film to be recognized.

…and I was the first guy to change Stereoscopic 3D to Digital 3D in 2008 with a film called 'Comin at Ya', a 3D hit of the early 80's. I actually thought that CAY would be a smash hit like it was in 81'…the first audience-participatory film I ever presented.

Could not find a distributor and today its still the best representation of 3D you will probably never see!

The only 3D Western on the planet.

'Ahead of your time' is overrated…I think its better to be 'on time' and as Stella Adler used to say all the time 'just do it'.

Horses

I have no idea when or where it started but somehow horses and I never got along. They just seem to know this and therefore are not crazy about me…they smell the whole ballgame, so to speak.

I think it began with a simple 'pony ride' at the Asbury Park boardwalk…when have you last heard of a kid that gets thrown off a 'pony-ride horse'?…the answer is never as these ponies are practically sleepwalking around the ring…how embarrassing to fall off a 'pony-ride horse' and have all the kids waiting in line laughing at you.

Anyway, it never bothered me, I just said no to riding horses and of course, every girl I was ever serious about, loved horses and asked me to go riding with them…no way!

Samantha was a horse in another life because when you saw her ride in a film, she looked like she and the horse were one…a beautiful flowing picture of rider and horse galloping thru the open landscape.

So, wouldn't you know it, my first role in a film was an 'Irish Teamster' on a wagon train carrying whisky…I had to learn to handle a four-horse wagon in a wagon-train… are you kidding me!!

They said 'don't worry, we got a Cowboy who is the best guy in Hollywood with horses…you will have no problem'

So, there I was, staring at a team of four horses (I didn't like one!…but four!) and the cowboy had me up in the wagon, showing me how to hold the reins and then I did what I was told…use the sound you make out of the side of your mouth…clic clic and giddy e yap and they moved…amazing!

Then they started to go faster and faster, not paying any attention to my pulling up on the reins and saying whoa!!...that's when the cowboy took over and guess what…the horses didn't give a shit who was holding the reins…they were heading out of here…except for one thing…we were in a big corral…uh oh!!

PANIC gripped the cowboy as he shouted 'get off'

I would except we were going pretty fast and I didn't...

The cowboy pushed me off the wagon...then he jumped as the horses and wagon crashed into the corral.

So, this was the 'best' cowboy to teach me and look what happened.

The Horse Guild had passed the word that this guy was just not crazy about them and they would teach me a lesson...horses and I just don't see eye to eye!!

My next encounter was 'the real deal'

The wagon train was all set up. I was to be driving the 8th wagon of a 20 wagon- train and the camera would pan down to me and my dialogue would begin...also, I was the 1st shot of the movie...no pressure!

They drove me to the eighth wagon which had four horses...NO problem as I had been taught by 'the best'... NOT!!

Anyway, the wagon-train started and all went well... I actually said 'whoa' and they stopped...nobody even picked up the fact that I was scared out of my mind!

Months after the film, I had occasion to meet Alex Cord, a bona-fide cowboy-actor who was on the rodeo circuit and I told him the story of my encounter with the four-horse wagon and he said that the 'Hollywood horses' only wanted the food and would turn on anyone not used to the way these horses behaved.

He said that when he had to do something that required horsemanship and he was using a Hollywood horse, he would just punch them in the mouth to get their attention before getting on them and everything was fine…I said 'you really punched them' and he just nodded and that was that!

He also told me to just admit I didn't like horses and for anything difficult, they would get a double to do the 'hard stuff' and so I did and no one ever said anything about it.

I never had any more problems with horses as I admitted my 'flaw' and they, in fact, got someone to do anything difficult so when I did my first 'Gunsmoke' they 'doubled' me and were very nice about it.

I did a second 'Gunsmoke' and this time, they doubled me and since I was always a 'bad guy' they varied the way I was killed. The first one they just shot me, the second one they hung me.

Then I got a third one and I actually new the director Dick Donner, who went on to do many big films. However on this Gunsmoke there was a ride written for me that was very, very, hairy and so I asked for a double and they said they would have one.

But on the night of the stunt, I arrived on set and everyone seemed excited.

Dick Donner asked how I felt and I replied fine...I looked around and it appeared that there was some joke or something going on...anyway Dick said to me.

'Look, I want you to take your horse out to those woods and when I say action, I want you to gallop as fast as you can toward the cabin and stop, jump off and take the letter into the cabin'

Why are you telling me this...where is the double?

No double this time Tom.

Are you out of your mind, you know I cant do that!

I look around and everyone is in on the joke and doubled up in laughter...everyone is laughing but ME!

Dick, you're joking right?

No, this is no joke…you were hired and this is what we need.

The realization is hitting me and frankly, I know I am headed for the hospital! 911 here I come.

OK, I say, I'll be back in a few, and with the laughter surrounding me, I head for my dressing room where I role the biggest 'joint' I can and smoke the whole thing… when I hit the ground, I will be relaxed or so I think.

Eventually, I come back to the set where everyone is smiling in anticipation of an actor getting killed…it must be like the Roman Coliseum as the patrons are drooling with anticipation.

I get on the horse and make my way to the woods… Dick said to waive when I am ready and he will say 'Action'.

When I am out of site of the camera, I get off my horse and move in front of the horse and with all my might, I punch the horse in the mouth and say "Do what I want… you fuck… or I am dead…do you understand…the horse is still shaking off the punch!

I get back on and move to where I can see the cabin and raise my hand…ACTION!

I kick the horse and urge him on to where I think I am going right through the damn cabin…

Pulling in on both reins, I slide in a cloud of dust stopping just in time… jump off and go into the cabin.

And I don't hear PRINT which indicates not having to do it again…

I put my head out the door and scream "that's a PRINT MOTHERFUCKER!!'

Everyone including Donner cheered.

I still have a problem with horses!!

Ba in Film (So, You Want to Make a MOVIE?)

Samantha and I were married about three years when I realized that my acting career had a problem concerning the quality of the parts I was getting. I realized that the roles I was being offered were just moving the story forward, but had nothing to do with a character with a beginning, middle, and end. And therefore were not exactly why I came into the 'biz' or maybe I was spoiled by my early success.

One of the problems was that as soon as Sam became pregnant with Nicolas, I turned down roles because they were geographically undesirable such as a lead in a TV series to be shot on the St. Lawrence river in Canada… in the winter!

So, when I got a call from Joe Solomon regarding the lead in a motorcycle film to be shot in Bakersfield, I said I'd do it. It was called 'Angels From Hell' and while it was not the best biker film to be made in that period...I figured I should not turn down any more work.

It was, in fact, one of the worst. You can tell it was the worst by going to youtube and typing in 'knife fight tom stern' and you will see me wielding a knife...a good laugh.

And if by chance you are not impressed with my 'macho', you will see me break the bad guy's leg on a curb...I just stomped him...him being 'the Alaskan Bear', a big, 280 lbs wrestler who was one of the nicest guys you ever want to meet...he could crush me with one hand tied behind him!

It was during the filming of this hard-R rated film that I had the idea of making a motorcycle film that a family could see. (up to this point there had not been any biker film made with an 'M' (mature) rating.

Jeremy Slate was in this film and one day we went out, under a tree and smoked a joint and I said to him that we should think of a story that a family could see and he suggested we play 'brothers' as we looked vaguely similar.

I said we had to have 'Angels' in the film to make it marketable and then I came up with the idea of using them to do something else.

Then it all came together: The brothers, being rich, would use the Angels to rob Caesars Palace in Vegas... the Angels would be blamed and we would escape back into our lives and secretly give the money to a good cause...brilliant!!...but of course we were 'stoned' so we would revisit this tomorrow to see if it still sounded feasible...

The next day we agreed to playing the brothers, he and I would get the story-by credit a I would Produce the film...I had a lot to do but I had to finish this film first...

THE PROCESS
Then my mind went crazy and thought of approaching Larry Gordon, my friend who was head of production at AIP (American International Pictures) and made all these exploitation films...but I am not quite ready!!

First, I had to get a screenplay written and I had to find an experienced writer to write a script...I searched for a writer that had written both biker and family and I found one that had worked for Disney and had written a biker film...Don Tait, who agreed to write this with my input and so, we were a go!

Although I had some experience, having had the production company Tracom with Stan Canter (another story) I had never done anything like this before, taking an idea to screenplay to the screen but I felt I could do this...

While the screenplay was being done, I kept thinking of the title when it hit me!

Use the original Oakland Hells Angels in the pic...shoot it in 68' and distribute it in 69'...call it Hells Angels 69!!

That night, after smoking some juana, I realized I knew a guy that was a minority partner in Caesars Palace and so I called him, I pitched the idea and he said to let him think about it.

Five minutes later he called.

He said he loved it and would get the hotel to approve all shooting in the building...and pick up all room expense related to the film...but we had to do it in the summer when biz was slow...

I said no problem, assuming I find the deal and the money!

He laughed.

PRODUCER
The hardest part about making a film is making the deal for the finance…its all about the deal!

Now I got Caesar's Palace and I got a screenplay coming and I got the 'stars' (Jeremy and myself)…so far, so good.

All I am missing is a finished screenplay, the distributor, the money to make the film and of course, the Angels!

No problem!

I also had a problem with the Angels. Supposing Sonny Barger doesn't like it, then the film is dead…Sonny is 'the man'!

It isn't easy to make a movie!...but if you can sell life insurance, you can sell anything!

The screenplay came in and with some changes…was ready to go!

I immediately called Gordon and made an appointment to pitch him the idea.

It was important to condense the story to one sentence, if possible…

So when I met Gordon, I said

'Two brothers use the Hells Angels to rob Caesars Palace of a half a million dollars'

His response was…

'If you get the Angels, we'll do it!'

Now the pressure was on.

I handed him the screenplay and left.

It was that fast!

Sonny Barger
Sonny was not only the head of the Oakland Chapter of the Hells Angels but was the head man of the entire Hells Angels network of chapters.

Believe it or not, in the 60's, Sonny had a listed number, so I called and he picked up the phone and I asked for a meeting to explain my movie idea and he said to come to Oakland, he would send someone to meet me.

I asked him how I would know the guy picking me up and he answered 'don't worry, you'll know him!'

So, I flew to Oakland and although the airport was filled, I noticed a long-haired, bearded guy with the 'colors' on and knew he had to be 'the guy'.

I was shocked to be picked up by a guy having a Cadillac Brome, a high quality car of that period, and he immediately offered me a 'joint'. He then offered me some blow, which I turned down.

We reached Sonny's house and I was shocked...it was nothing like I would have pictured. It was a nice, ranch-style house with boxes of rhododendrons (little red flowers) in each of the front windows. And of course, it had a picket fence. You would have thought an average American lived here...wrong!...and I learned soon enough that all preconceptions of the 'Angels' would turn out to be wrong!

I entered to find Sonny sitting around a large oval table with all the recognizable Angels that you have seen in the papers...notably Terry the Tramp, Animal, Tiny, and Magoo.

The table had several bowls on it filled with Reds (downers), Whites (uppers), Joints (marijuana)...in addition, each had their weapon of choice on the table for me to see!

Everyone wants to make a film but I knew I would be tested…they called it 'holding your mud'…the 'ride' and all this shit on the table was the beginning…

Told them that I wanted to make a biker film that kids could see and that would be a 'first'!…they smiled…so I thought I would get the "real bikers who happen to be you and call the film 'Hells Angels 69'

They liked that.

Then I suggested that maybe we use half from here and maybe half from San Francisco, if Sonny thought that would be ok…

Sonny said, 'why don't you take him over there… they'll be partying!'

And boom, Terry the Tramp and Tiny get up and point to me and say 'lets go' and we pile into the 'Brome' and off we go over the Oakland Bay Bridge to SF Angel party!

The party was happening as there were a whole bunch of Angels dancing and drinking and dancing and drinking…the place was packed! The smell of 'juana' in da air!

I was not very comfortable, but I tried to stay calm. I was intro'd to the #1 of SF Angels and I told him the story and he seemed ok with the idea.

The SF Angels looked nothing like the guys I was with…as I am thinking about the casting the #1 comes up to me…I am now very nervous as I felt something was about to happen!

"My old lady wants you" he said. And when he said that, it turned weird…here is this beautiful girl that was standing next to him and he is giving her to me…what is really going on!!

If I say 'great'…he'll kill me!

If I say 'no thanks'…he will think 'what, she isn't good enough for you' and definitely kill me!

I stood there for what seemed like a long time and realized I had to react…so…

I went with the girl.

When we came back, everyone acted like this was another day in the park, so to speak. Nothing was said and eventually we left.

Everybody was pretty loaded. While laughing hysterically, they actually started to shoot out the lights on the bridge. I am sitting in the front as they start shooting.

Am I going to get a shot to the back of the head, like the Godfather movies… it starts to pour…so now the windows are open and the rain is pouring in as they are still trying to shoot out the lights…OMG!

When we reach Sonny's, Terry the Tramp tells me to come with him… on his 'chopper' for a ride… in the rain…r u kidding me! I think 'what the fuck…'

Riding behind Terry the Tramp in the rain, is a breathtaking adventure in keeping your eyes tightly shut and praying silently that he gets tired of seeing if I 'hold my mud' and goes home!

I haven't been this scared since they put me in the front car of the 'Cyclone' on Coney Island!…I am not feeling good about the whole experience!

The Deal

My idea was always to only use the Oakland club. The next day I made a deal with Sonny based on my getting a deal from the distributor, AIP.

Larry Gordon, the Head of Production at AIP, couldn't believe I got the Angels and he offered me their standard deal, the one that all 'first timers' are given…"Half the money for half the world"… $250,000 of $500,000.

This may sound good but it's the worst deal you could possibly make…how is the other half going to get their moola back? They aren't.

I turn him down. Then I say 'Half the money for the US only'. Gordon reluctantly agrees. Then I go out and try to find the other half…this turns out to be a daunting task as I am turned down by everyone until I run into Pat Rooney. Rooney is an Executive Producer connected to Dell Webb, a large real estate developer, who likes to be the last one in and the first one out, so to speak. This means that they don't really want to put up the money, they just want to guarantee the $250,000.

So, I decide to make the film on the dollars given to me by AIP ($250,000) and use Rooney/Webb only if I absolutely have too. That way we can own half of domestic and all of foreign and if I go over, Rooney will come in to finish the film.

He became the Executive Producer and we went out and hired a Director. I gave myself the story credit along with Jeremy.

Las Vegas was a problem in that the Sheriff didn't want the Angels in Vegas so we had to find somewhere that would duplicate Caesars Palace. We could shoot the 'heist' in the hotel but all exteriors had to be done somewhere else.

PRE-PRODUCTION
One day, I was in my office at 9000 Sunset, when Sonny and Terry walked in and emptied a paper bag on my desk…'we're in'!

I had never seen that much cash before… but I definitely could use it.

We budgeted and storyboarded the film prior to actually scheduling, but we all agreed to do all the desert work first. That would be in the Mojave Desert

The shooting went surprisingly well until the last day where upon returning to set, Jeremy Slate, riding his bike, stuck out his foot and promptly broke his leg!!…shit!

End of production…maybe…suspend production…definitely!!…how long?…who knows.

THE WORST DAY OF SHOOTING EVER!

As soon as we realized Jeremy would be in a cast and could stand up, we hired a new crew which we wanted to do anyway, and pushed back the production by only 1 week.

We were lucky that we completed the climax of the screenplay which took place in the desert.

I had placed a call to a friend and gotten a very accomplished Production Manager, Clark Paylow. Ten years later he would manage 'Close Encounters of a Third Kind', but this week he was going to help get us 'over the hump'…so to speak!

The morning went well with Jeremy just turning slightly for us to be able to cut to another shot. We finished the work several hours over the schedule but were extremely happy to have filmed at all…the new crew was infinitely better than the original one.

We now moved over to the Angel clubhouse and Jeremy was being chauffeured by an African-American in the car given to him by the Angels…the Cadillac Brome.

The new crew started to walk toward the clubhouse as the 'Brome' pulled in and parked in front of the house... the Angels had been drinking and smoking juana and we were late to the location.

As they approached all hell broke loose!!
The driver started running across the field followed by the Angels in pursuit...the new crew ran from the scene, Jeremy was knocked over, breaking his cast...

In the midst of this melee, an Angel, came up to me and asked to talk to me...I said ok and he led me into the house and into a room where I heard him lock the door...the click of the door locking jarred me into a 'fear' I had never experienced before...I was about to be killed!

When Sonny heard about it, he ran into the clubhouse shouting for help...then banging on the door, trying to save me...they finally broke the door down...by that time I had a black eye, a puffed lip and contusions up and down my body...not a good look for a leading man!

They took me back to the production office, everyone was aghast at the site of their Producer/Star and just then, Pat Rooney appeared and after seeing me, ordered the Production shut down period...he said 'this film is finished'...wrap it up!

I went nuts, got up, grabbed Rooney, lifted him up and put him against the wall and said 'I'll tell you when we are finished, and this film goes on till I say so…do you understand?'…he sheepishly nodded!

So, Sonny saved me and I saved the film!!

'Somebody has to fix me up, I have to appear in front of the town council of Mountain View'.

Everyone looked at me as if to say 'put him in a padded cell!'

I have to convince them that we were a 'non-violent motorcycle film with the Hells Angels!! …quiet laughter!

We had to film tomorrow, so that night, with a cane and dark glasses, I appeared at the meeting because that was the only day they would give me!

IF I could convince them…I figured IF could get them to laugh at me…I might get a good outcome!

I apologized to the council for my appearance but I had had a motorcycle accident and frankly, was thankful that I could even appear…they smiled sort of!

Then I told them that I wanted to be the first producer to do a non-violent motorcycle film (giggling) and I thanked them for their consideration.

I would only film in the morning and would be gone by 11AM.

The council voted 7-6 in my favor and we started to film the next morning…the film had as the leads, a guy in a cast and another that couldn't show his face…a unique film!

Hells Angels 69' became a classic because it was the first biker film with an 'M' rating (PG-13) and the only one with the 'Original Oakland Hells Angels' in it.

In conclusion, I would tell anyone that asked, the Angels were 'pros'…they showed up on time, knew their lines and behaved, for the most part, like any other actors on the set of a film. Without them, there would have been no film at all…

Thank you Angels and a special thanks to Sonny!

The Whole Shabang

THE WEDDING

Well, I finally arrived for the wedding and Sam told me that I had to go to the church to get the priest's permission to marry. In order to get married in the Catholic persuasion, I had to promise to bring the children up "Catolic". So, I had to meet with a priest who explained to me what I had to sign!

I looked at him and said, does Jesus Christ and God know our every thought?

To which he replied, "of course". I looked at him, smiled, and agreed to bring up our children Catholic! The Priest knew he had been had!

Then we all went to the dinner prior to the wedding. David Rosen hired a room at a very fancy restaurant in London and planned the entire meal, sent the invitations, and arranged for beautiful flowers to be on the table! The four course meal was a gourmet's delight featuring an entree of roast beef.

David forgot only one thing, and that was that Sam was a vegetarian! There was nothing for her to eat! Sam ate a potato on her wedding eve.

The wedding was beautiful. Sam and I knelt in front of the Priest and everything went perfectly until the priest asked us to repeat the vows after him. One of the vows took so long that I lost track of what he was saying and said something like 'excuse me'

Apparently it was a funny moment, because both Peter and Paul had to leave the church to get themselves together!

We went to the reception, changed clothes and were driven to the airport in a powder-blue rolls. We left for New York and spent our first night at the Plaza Hotel. Of course Peter had screwed up the reservation and we couldn't have the bridal suite, but by turning the beds around, we managed to have a comfortable night!

We had breakfast in bed, got dressed and left for the airport and a plane to Albuquerque, N.M.

Arrived in Gallup on Sunday night to find that they weren't going to need me for several days!

After I got thru the urge to kill someone, and the jet-lag, we had a good time...sort of!

THE PROBLEM
Most people don't know this but Sam was in fact 'owned' by three British gentleman, which surprisingly was the norm for young budding actresses at that time. This was a business arrangement whereby Sam would be paid enough for rent and food and transportation, and they would get all monies she would earn forever!...a sort of 'servant contract'.

Columbia at the time wanted a long term contract with one of their 'stars', and as Sam was just starting out, it seemed like a good deal. But I soon realized that she needed help negotiating from a legal position in addition to a business manager. So I contacted Sidney Cohn, one of showbiz' biggest attorneys and he suggested Alexander Tucker, a well-respected business manager.

Three months later, we were at a cocktail party and a Producer came up to me and complained about being unable to close a deal for Sam. I asked him how much was involved and he replied $100,000. I was stunned. This was a great deal of money and a very big deal in 1965, as very few actors were making that kind of money.

I told the Producer that I would get back to him in three days with an answer.

So, a conference call was arranged with the three British gentleman that owned her and I gave them the great news that Sam has been offered $100,000 for a film and listened as they congratulated themselves and then asked when the film would start.

I told them that I had turned the film down…they went nuts!…what do you mean you turned it down?

Look, I said, I saw how little money she got for doing the Collector and frankly, I am not going to let anyone 'own' her…period!…I want to buy her out of the contract.

They put their hand over the phone and I could hear them arguing…they came back with 'ok, we'll take half and cancel the contract'.

I replied 'you will take 25% and I want an answer now!'

They agreed and Sam was a 'free' woman.

The Strategy

I called Sidney who congratulated me and I explained to him that Sam was in a 'unique' position of being able to avoid taxes in the US and England by not living in either place for six months...he said he would check it with Tucker and get back to me.

And so began our moving every six months or so and Sam establishing an Offshore account. In the winter we stayed in Zurs, one of the great skiing resorts in all of Switzerland...this back and forth worked for awhile!

We lived in some incredible houses in those first years. The one I remember the most was on Maple Dr. because it was so luxurious. We had this great pool in the back and big lawns all around.

But what I remember the most about the Maple house was Christmas when Nicolas turned 1yr old.

Sam was a big star and on Christmas, everyone and I mean everyone and everyone's secretary and everyone's assistant want to make sure they are recognized and appreciated by Sam, so they all send presents...

Hold on, wait a minute...you don't understand!

Nicolas had over one-hundred presents under the tree...are you kidding me...the poor kid was tired of opening presents...it took him three days!

And those were just for Nicolas...there were another hundred for Sam!

It was totally embarrassing and we decided to give away ALL presents the following year if this continued and we did!

And then came Jenna and all that changed...we had to find a home and we did. Sam bought a house in Brentwood with a porch which I loved.

But our problems persisted until I started and finished shooting HA 69.

ON THE ROCKS
After the production of HA 69 which was shot in 68', we came to the conclusion that our marriage was in 'deep trouble'. Sam decided that she would make a decision in London where she was going to make a film and she would take the kids with her...this was in early 69'. By that time, she was being repped by Freddie Fields at CMA.

I used to play racquetball every afternoon at the Beverly Hills Men's Club and frequently played with Paul Caruso, a killer defense lawyer very well known in town. He invited me to his office the next morning to discus the problem.

I told him, "Freddie is a lying son of a bitch and I don't trust him for a minute, but Sam likes him." I had a lot more to say about Freddie but I let it be…

I continued, "If she decides to divorce me in London, I'm fucked and will never see my kids again…I don't mean never, its just that the British laws don't favor the father so, there is a good chance that it will be difficult to see them…and I want to see them as much as possible!"

Paul thought about the problem for a moment and replied, "There is only one way to accomplish your goals and frankly, I don't think you will like it:

You will have to get an injunction stopping her from leaving the country with the children and frankly, it will be big news and will hit all the papers everywhere.

Paramount and Columbia will hate you and so will all her advisors and friends but this is the ONLY way!

The kids will be 'wards of the court' so she can take them anywhere but she must bring them back!

By the way, you can kiss your career goodbye as well.

So, go home and think about it and let me know tomorrow…I don't envy you."

For me this was a 'no brainer'…my kids were the 'whole ballgame' to me and I knew I could handle all the bullshit that was gonna come my way, so the next day I called Paul and gave him the 'green light'.

He was right about everything. We were on the front page around the world…I was threatened by everybody including both studios, her agents, publicists, friends and so many more people that I didn't know BUT our divorce was over in twenty-four hours…for a new Cali record!

Although I helped create her money, I wanted none of it…I just wanted to see the kids fifty percent of the time and she agreed…so it was over…Sam got on the plane with the kids and headed for London.

Within a year, I received apologies from everyone that had chastised me.

Juana Boy

The first time I smoked weed was in Greenwich Village and I knew for sure I was high when I realized I had driven the wrong way for two blocks on a one-way street!! Hello!

I was also twenty-one and had just moved into Greenwich Village, when I was invited to a party and was handed a joint!...I coughed my brains out until someone showed me how to smoke a joint inhaling very slowly.

After that I smoked occasionally but never really got into it until I got to California in 1964.

I do remember a jazz band in Germany made up of black soldiers, who went around smoking pipes... I never liked pipes so I asked them why they all had them and they laughed and laughed. Then they took me to an empty lot in the middle of Frankfurt which was still all torn apart from World War ll. As I looked at the overgrown lot in between half torn-down buildings, they said that the whole lot was marijuana...oh, the pipes, got it!!

In the middle of the 60s', all the good weed in California had a yellow look to it...it was called Acapulco Gold and there was a story about a mystical guy that drove his jeep over the border fences or brought it in on speedboats... they called him 'Juana Boy'...they say he supplied all the stars in Hollywood including the studio heads with the best weed...

One night I went to The Daisy to mess around, play pool and have some fun. There was this guy I met that after the game asked me if I would like to join him for a joint. After one toke I knew it was the 'gold' and I asked him where he got it, I would like to buy some. He just gave me some joints and said that he would get me some.

That was the beginning of a long friendship with the 'Juana Boy' David Wheeler, who among his many accomplishments, was able to roll a joint as he raced his silver Porsche along Sunset Boulevard while changing gears and talking to you with no hands on the steering wheel!...scary!

This guy knew everyone and everyone thought they knew who he was...but in the end, no one actually knew who he was or what he did for a living.

They thought he was a 'dealer' of weed, cocaine and other hallucinogens while others thought he was a CIA operative…some knew him as a botanist who worked with UCLA.

You see, DW was in fact all the above and more.

He actually was the son of a State Department Ambassador and spoke at least three languages and carried a 'red passport', which allowed him to bring in 'anything' he wanted thru customs without any examination what-so-ever…so he would just bring in a suitcase of 'Peruvian' blow with no problem!

He carried a silver .45 at all times and was lover of 'fighting knives', going to the far ends of wilderness country to find a certain 'knife maker'.

It was said he was a Mafia member because his California plants started to show up all around the country.

The entire drug culture changed and it was rumored to be because of the 'Juana Boy'. He was a 'brilliant' botanist who developed most of the new strains of juana working both in the UCLA labs which had a division that no one knew about, that mixed the seeds of various plants to give different 'highs'.

David would then take the seeds to the botanists at Harvard who would test the seeds as they were concerned with 'delivery systems' used to treat asthma, emphysema and other bronchial conditions...the beginning of vaporizers developed by 'Juana boy'.

From the time I met David, he was 'growing' on farms out in the areas that were best for growing: dry areas in the San Fernando valley as far north as the Ojai area and then down to Rainbow, just north of Escondido.

He trained pit bulls to guard the fenced-in crop against the thieves who prowled the countryside looking to steal a crop.

He had to move each season as the Feds were always after him and just as they got close, he and his friend David Astor would pull all the plants and be gone in the middle of the night...they were modern day outlaws!

In the world of marijuana, Juana Boy was a super-star, being featured in 'High Times' three times.

I gave them the monikers of David North (Astor) and David South (Wheeler) and they both were frequent visitors to my Rangely St. railroad apartment, that is to say, the rooms went straight back one after the other. They used to use my guest room to stay during the week.

I would sometimes hear them argue over the amount of money they had just received for a 'crop'. The problem was that they were so 'loaded', they could never get the same amount so as they argued, I laughed…if I could of only filmed it!

The world of 'Juana' used to hold a contest each year in Amsterdam called the 'Cannabis Cup'… This was way before the various states in the US approved the growing and selling of 'Juana'. David South was to be honored one year and he invited me to join him as he had two tickets and just wanted some company. So I went with him.

As far as the folk in Amsterdam were concerned, 'Juana Boy' walked on water! He was a star! David was an 'original' and knew every strain and seed shown to him and he could explain how to get the most product out of each seed.

This was the beginning of the ever-growing seed business that went around the world and now supplies all the different names of Juana you hear about…it all started with 'Juana Boy'.

South would visit me in San Diego many times and on one occasion, I noticed him limping a bit. He said that his leg was bothering him, sometimes swelling up and that he thought he had 'gout', a possible circulatory problem…so I insisted he see a heart specialist and he agreed.

I called one of the best in the country that I had met playing tennis. He said to have him come in immediately and he did. He told David that he needed an operation on his leg to alleviate any circulatory problem. He didn't have to do it today, but within 90 days.

Sixty days later, David was coming back from Vancouver with 300 grand in a backpack and while staying overnight at a motel with his girlfriend of the moment, had a heart attack and died in bed. She called 911 and the Police showed up to investigate. The cash went "missing".

There were at least fifty people at his funeral and everyone said something about David and not one person said the same thing…fifty totally different stories about 'Juana Boy'…you would have thought that fifty different people had died!!

This guy left a big imprint on this world!…loved the guy!

MBA in Film

What defines an MBA in film?

Well, the easy way is to go to USC or Northwestern or some other accredited university and go thru the normal way after getting your BA (Bachelor of Arts)

On the other hand, there is another way to achieve the necessary accreditation to fulfill the requirements and you be the judge…

After finishing Hells Angels 69, I was divorced from Samantha and found a place on Horn St. in Hollywood, just above Tower Records and in the middle of the action on the Sunset Strip.

Having gone thru, what some might describe as the most difficult film ever (Hells Angels 69), I was hungry to find a film to do and started to read everything in sight.

One night at The Daisy, I ran into a friend of mine who told me about Ron Buck, the guy that owned 9000 Sunset. Apparently he was a non-published writer that was dabbling in screenplay writing and had a screenplay that was making 'the rounds'.

Since I read as much as possible, I asked to read it and my friend said he would ask Ron if he would allow me to see it…

Although the screenplay was a bit rough, the story of a Vet returning from the ugly war in Vietnam who just wanted to be left alone, sell scrap metal on the streets to make 'enough' to survive…intrigued me!

The fact that the DEA would use this vet to capture a drug lord without his consent was even better.

The fact that the vet had fallen over a grenade in order to save his company and the grenade failed to go off was even more enticing because his life was now 'borrowed'…so to speak.

It was very edgy, subversive material—*especially for the time*—so I just went for it.

Seeing myself playing the vet was an added enticement…I got word to Buck that I was interested in producing the film and things progressed from there and we made the deal.

The first thing I did was 'find the moola'…a Canadian millionaire invited me to Vancouver to talk to him and we got along just fine. I knew this would work out when he offered me a 'joint'. He agreed to put up $600,000 and we started the paperwork. We were a go!

Based on having the money, I talked to Jack Gilardi at ICM and he suggested Telly Savalas for the lead bad-guy to play the CIA operative.

Once I had him, I got Burgess Meredith, Robert Vaughn, John Marley, Ivan Dixon and cast Marilyn Akin (my girlfriend at the time) as the girl and we were off and running…hired a Director…and my friend Frank Avianca as an assistant producer.

I set a start date six weeks away and went into pre-production. Ron Buck gave me office space in the 9000 Sunset which was two blocks from my house on Horn.

Hired an assistant Laura Fey as we started the process…

We got all the locations including the Hollywood Bowl for the climax of the film. All the actors were signed and cleared thru Screen Actors Guild…I was feeling pretty good.

Two weeks out, I checked the bank and the $600,000 had not been deposited…no problem…the funds were coming from Canada so maybe tomorrow.

Tomorrow came and went and now I am worried but I don't show it…it will work out… I thought…

Its 9PM and I am going crazy. I cant wait another minute, so I call my Canadian who, after the usual greeting, informs me that because of several tax problems, he has to back out of the deal!

Back out of the deal…what the fuck are you talking about, we start this film in two weeks…I'll lose everything!

I'm sorry he says and BOOM…he hangs up!

…I am crushed…and numb…I could sue him but he lives in Canada…impossible!!

I have a problem…a big problem…huge!! the actors are 'pay or play' so that means I owe them their salaries.

So, there I am, smoking a joint with Frank, discussing my options…

'You don't have any'!!…Frank was ripped and… we laughed!

This is impossible…I have two weeks and I don't have the money so, first thing I do is review the cash flow needed week by week. The next thing I do is smoke a fatty, turn up the music and float thru the morning…

I had just completed the most difficult film ever and now…I just don't give up, I never have and this will NOT be the first…

I made the decision that by hook or by crook, I was going to make this film and I tell no one except Frank and Laura Fey. I would produce and act during the day and take meetings at night to raise the cash necessary for that week.

I did that for five of the six weeks we were shooting, sleeping about four hours a night and then…they caught up with me…SAG was sending a bunch of execs to my office to close the film down until certain monies were paid to SAG…meanwhile we kept on shooting.

Got a call from Laura Fey that the SAG folk were in the office. I told her to set them up in the conference room, give them coffee and I will be right over.

There were five guys in suits and a nicely dressed lady, as I came into the room. Then they started to tell me all the trouble I was in and how much money I needed to come up with in order for them not to shut me down... and each person said something worse than the other... (I wished I had a camera to shoot this!!)

I had been thru this 'you cant do this' experience many times, and they were going to shut me down...I don't think so...I asked them if they were finished and they all nodded in the affirmative...I then told them to get the fuck out of my office and now! I meant it...I never saw them again!

I was desperate; I had no money, the credit cards were maxed out and I had another week of shooting and I needed funds to finish the editing...I finally called Sidney Cohn, my friend and attorney to the stars. He said he would see what he could do...he was also the attorney for MGM and eventually, he figured it out and came up with the money and distribution...just lucky, I guess!!

We had gotten to the point in the schedule that demanded speed or we would never make it...period! We had only one more week and one day to shoot the Hollywood Bowl...

I made a Producer's decision and replaced the Director who I thought could not finish in time.

I took over the directing and my first scene was directing Burgess Meredith who gave me my initiation…messing up lines, coughing, and generally fucking up three 'takes'…loved that man.

We only had a day to shoot the Hollywood Bowl, so I went there and planned the entire shoot including every camera position for three cameras moving from the top of the stadium all the way to the stage…and I was going to have Yogi Bashan and one-hundred of his followers on stage…chanting!!

Let's see, I am Producing, Directing and starring in the film…I have averaged four hours of sleep for the last six weeks…it's the climax* of the film and I am loving the process…this was a real test, one that I accepted against all odds.

We finished on time and on budget.

*This scene of the film available at www.aspenwood-publishing.com

Music

After the film had been edited, we went to MGM to score the film. I had already gotten the rights to Arlo Guthrie's 'I Could Be Singing' and Taj Mahal's 'Ain't Gonna Whistle Dixie Anymore', and others but I was having trouble with the soundtrack over certain scenes.

Anyway, one day I went to pick up the kids at Sam's house. As I was waiting, Jenna (4yo) said that Kriboffilin was coming…I said who? And as she was about to answer, the doorbell rang and since I was standing near it, I opened it to find Kris Kristofferson standing there.

I said, hi, I'm the ex just picking up the kids and he was very nice as we waited…not to miss this opportunity, I told him that I had been trying to get the rights to use 'Law is For Protection of the People' for my film, about a vet back from Vietnam, and was turned down.

He said, what are you going to use it for and I said 'do you want to see just how I want to use it... I'm at MGM and would love you to see the film...

He said 'sure' and so the following week, I showed him the scene and he loved it and said 'you got it' and better yet, they wont charge you a cent...couldn't have been nicer.

Well, that takes care of the Hollywood Blvd scene... but the climax...I don't know!

One weekend I take the kids up into Topanga Canyon to visit a friend of David Wheeler (juana boy) and we all went over to his friend's place which sat atop a meadow in the middle of nowhere.

The kids went out and played in the meadow.

His friend and his friends played string instruments and improvised as they went along...I had never heard anything like this...it was eerie and beautiful at the same time.

MGM was known for doing very large films with a full orchestra that played in a stadium-like studio on the MGM lot...and that's where they were going to mix my score...they did Arlo's songs and Kris Kristofferson's song and then they asked how I was going to do the final scene.

I told them that I would like to try a 'string quartet' and they looked at me like I had lost my mind...a quartet?...we have a full orchestra here and you want to use a quartet?

Okay, what music will they play?

I said, 'I don't know yet'...they looked at each other and then said 'we will need some time to acquaint everyone with the music'.

I said, 'no, you wont, because they are going to improvise the music...they are going to see what is going on up on the screen and improvise the score...

They were speechless!

Mr. Stern, we don't do things this way, so maybe you would like to talk to our execs.

I said, hold on, we are just trying something...if it doesn't work, we will do whatever you suggest...they agreed.

So, in comes these bearded hippie musicians and set up their instruments: a bass, a viola, a violin, and a steel guitar.

When they are ready and the engineers are ready, we roll the entire Hollywood Bowl sequence including the 'chanting' from Yogi Bashan group. The guys just played while watching the whole ending of the film.

We then played it back while watching the film…

The execs were astounded…the music was extraordinary…they had never seen anything like this and complimented me on my choice…they were musically blown away!!

The Film

Well, the film was finished and we just waited for someone to tell us when we would have a screening in order to judge what the hell we had…

We heard nothing…this went on for several months with various excuses…finally, I went over to the studio and demanded a screening. I told them that I realize that I had made a very different film and that they had come in at the end, but we should see if anyone likes it…they agreed and told me they would find a screening time for us.

I had this feeling of an orphan who has just been brought into a new family….they really didn't want me but there I was…

So I was shocked to hear from them that they were going to screen the film in Beverly Hills at midnight, just after 'Mad Dogs and Englishman'.

Midnight! …I wasn't thrilled…Call me arrogant but I wasn't thrilled about the first showing of the film to be behind anything!...much less these guys!

So, we all went and got there towards the end of Mad Dogs and I noticed about six or seven 'suits' all in a row as the first film finished.

They waited for several minutes and started Clay Pigeon.

The film starts as Arlo Guthrie plays over a platoon going thru some marshland…obviously Vietnam!

A guy throws a grenade and one of the soldiers shouts 'grenade' and then falls over the grenade to save the platoon…and it doesn't go off!!!

The crowd goes nuts standing and clapping…I cant believe it!!

They do this six times during the film including a final standing ovation at the end credits…they loved it!

Afterwards, I go back to see the executives, who are totally bewildered…they tell me that they have never seen anything like this before at a screening.

We are going to screen this again, they say and leave...

I stood there shaking my head...six standing ovations...at a movie...unbelievable!!

BEGINNING OF THE END

The next screening was in Lakewood in Orange County. They screened the film without any advertising and of course there was very few people there...there was no reaction to the film...good or bad...and that's not good.

The normal way to distribute a film in that time frame was to open in one theater on the weekend and expand the amount of theaters the next week and again the following week...then at a later date, open the film wide... but the first Fri grosses of the 'exclusive engagement' went out all over the country and that would determine the outcome of the film.

I tried to find out how they planned to distribute but could get no commitment...I waited and waited and then...

They said they were going to open in a theater in Boston on the July 4th weekend...

I just didn't understand…who stays in the city on the July 4th weekend…nobody that's who…

Telly or Burgess could help open the film but they weren't even invited.

The only trailer that ran, ran in that theater only.

Fri grosses were dismal…we were done in 'the exclusive' in one night!

Then they went 'wide' in the Drive-in's in the Southeast… in the fall…

The only competition was the Fri night high school football games, the Saturday college football games and the Sun pro-football games and oh, I forgot, Baseball was still being played!! (And that's why nobody goes out with a film in the fall)

The film died. MGM never even made a video deal for the film, so nobody has seen it yet!!

I was told that because the film was so 'political' (pro-marijuana, anti-government) they decided to just kill it!

Several years later I was told that the CIA had a guy at every studio including MGM who were paid by the CIA to weed out anti-government films about Vietnam and destroy them...legally!

And that was my MBA...

Charlie

The other night I woke up thinking about the name Charlie and how significant this name has been in my life. My Grandson now has the great name of Charlie.

One of the short stories in this book is titled 'But He's George To Me' and refers to my relationship to George Abbott, one of the icons of Broadway, who directed me in the London Company of Never To Late. My role's name was Charlie.

Since I met Samantha while in the play, the name has come full circle without anyone even knowing the significance.

When I spoke to my Daughter-in-law and Charlie's mom Mindy, she told me that they 'just liked the name' and didn't give Charlie a middle name or initial because neither her father 'Sol' or her husband Nicolas, or his father Tom have a middle name or initial.

And all of this comes from my father 'Harry S. Stern' who somehow never told me why he hated his middle name 'Stanley' but obviously hated it because my name is Tom, not Thomas, and no middle name…Dad must have had issues not discussed!

Although "Charlie" isn't a family name perse, it has a history in our family. When the kids were little I had this game I would play while I drove them crosstown to school on Monday mornings. It was called 'ZX4 TO CONTROL TOWER'.

I was the pilot of this plane taking the kids to school… and the control tower was run by a guy called 'Charlie'. It would go something like this:

ZX4 to Control Tower…nothing

ZX4 to Control Tower…come in Charlie…Charlie, u there?

Control Tower to ZX4…this is Charlie…do you ZX4 have a problem

Charlie, I need an update on the weather situation…cause I cant see shit here!

Laughter starts…bad dad…swears in front of his children…and it begins…it becomes hysterical as 'bad dad' goes off with Charlie and is only stopped by the kid in the back (Nicolas) who cant keep it together and pukes out the rear window…and then continues to laugh.

Thanks to my Grandson the name Charlie will now always be a family name!

Summers

Have no idea how I became the 'pied piper of kids' but I did…it seemed that wherever I went, the kids would just come to me. They must have sensed that even though I was bigger, and of course older, that beneath the exterior was a 'kid' waiting to play with them. And I fully admit that I would rather be with kids than grown-ups.

It was nothing but pure laughter. That was my 'drug of choice' and still is to this day. Today I am helping coach a bunch of 13 year olds and it seems in retrospect, that I have been coaching or playing all my life.

When I would enter The (Ocean) Beach Club, it was embarrassing as all the kids would run to me and I would have to wrestle them off just to enter the club. I am talking about 15 to 20 kids…that's right, I would be on the bottom of the pile of these kids and I would extricate myself with hysterical laughter bubbling over from all. It truly was a sight and it would go on in or out of the water. It was the 'pied piper gene' and it must have come from Ros.

In the water, I would throw them everywhere and only the parents were a bit nervous. I knew I would never hurt anyone…they loved it!

So naturally, when I finally thought of marriage, which was when I reached my 30s', the thought of a family was the deciding factor.

And although I had been with some incredible looking women in my life, the first time I saw Samantha Eggar was a 'bolt of lightning' moment. I knew immediately that I wanted her as a wife and mother: The children would be spectacular and they were…are!

Loving your wife is one thing, but nothing compares to the love of children and I can attest to that. I wanted to spend as much time with them as possible…acting was great and hitting a baseball was great and making love was great. BUT the time spent with my children took precedent over all else.

Samantha and I got divorced when the kids were 4 and 2 years old. The first summer was strange because Samantha didn't think I could do it myself so I had to take the 'nanny' with me to the house I rented on the beach in Malibu.

I had the kids every available 'free' moment for most of their childhood and I loved it…(seven straight years of every week-end and every vacation both winter and summer...I cant begin to tell you what we did, but we laughed a lot. I began taking them somewhere every summer.

To digress for a moment, the second I hit London, I fell totally in love with the place. The first time was when I was in the service of my country (joke) in late '56. Then I got the role of 'Charlie' in 'Never Too Late' which played at the 'Price of Wales' in Piccadilly, the heart of London. I was on stage when Kennedy was assassinated in '63.

Anyway, after my divorce, every chance I got, I went to London and on one of my 'run-aways' I met Sandra, an amazing woman with two children the same ages as my two. Sandra thought we should all go away together and she knew a farmhouse in Minorca that we could rent for six weeks. I thought that was a fabulous idea so the next summer, we all went to Minorca, a small island in the Mediterranean...amazing!!

Imagine going to a different beach every day for a month, eating picnics, one better that the other as Sandra was an incredible cook who spoiled me for life... she was that good! We lived in a farmhouse surrounded by other farms and in the morning, the other farmers would leave veggies or eggs or whatever meat they had slaughtered, on the patio for us…and the best part was that there were no bugs on that island…that's right…zip, nada, zero bugs…unbelievable! Sleeping outside on the patio, under the stars was a truly unique experience… tough to even imagine… no bugs! A wow moment!

One weekend I took Nicolas to the Taormina Film Festival where I won 'Best Actor' for my film, 'Clay Pigeon." I used to tell everyone that my kids slept anywhere, anytime and I illustrated this by telling them about Nicolas, who went to sleep in the Barcelona Airport on our return. We were stuck till dawn, so N lay down on a wooden bench and went promptly to sleep. At least fifteen German Tour Buses full of drunken, singing, shouting tourists arrived and partied all around us…he never even knew they were there…unreal!…I didn't sleep a wink!

Another summer we went to the Jersey Shore and I took them to the Ocean Beach Club which they loved… we spent a month or so in Jersey where they met some of my old friends who told them stories about their father. We played ball on the front lawn, tried the 'dogs' at Max's and generally had a great time…in fact, several years later, we returned and took a house near Monmouth Beach on the Shore…as you can tell, we liked the beach so…

The next summer we went to Kauai, where we had a wonderful house on the beach. I was seeing a girl named Jody at the time, so I took Jody and her sister to help with the house/kids.

I hadn't started to surf yet but I did bodysurf and the best beach in the world for bodysurfing was in Poipu called Breneke Beach, a scant five minutes away. The kids took tennis lessons and swam.

As I bodysurfed Breneke on a big day, about a month into our stay, the farmers were burning the sugar cane fields and smoke was everywhere. When I came down a big wave and reached the beach, I could not get my breath…I was in trouble…they took me to a hospital and was given three shots of adrenalin that did nothing…so I made the decision to leave the islands.

So, we packed up the house and went to the airport ASAP, where I ever so slowly went up the stairs to the plane, one step at a time, because, one, I could hardly breathe and two, I was afraid they wouldn't let me fly…(note: it was '77' and they knew nothing about asthma in the islands. I was hoping I would last till I got to LA. I got off the plane and went immediately to the Century City Hospital, where I had been several times before and in a matter of hours, I was fine…that summer was sure different!

Another summer we rented a house in Rustic Canyon, an almost secret canyon way back off of Santa Monica Blvd that had a reputation as a 'refuge to the stars' and the only way I could rent this house was if I took care of their St. Bernard and another dog...Mashi and Lupa... the kids loved the dogs (they weren't much bigger than the dog) and I organized a baseball league that played in the Rustic Canyon Park...we were the 'Green Machine' and won, naturally...the beach is within walking distance but they also had a pool in the Canyon so good times were had by all. We had so much fun there that we did it again the following year.

I coached Nicolas from the time he was 6 through Little League at 13 and Jenna played from 6 through Little League at 13...they were both good players. Nicolas was a catcher and Jenna played 2nd base.

They also watched Dad play at Barrington Park, where one day I hit a ball off Bill Cosby over the right field fence and into a couple's living room on the 6th floor. The man stomped down with the ball in his hand demanding to know who had hit it. I came forward and the man, Sydney, smiled and congratulated me. He ended up inviting me and the kids to come to their pool where he and his wife allowed the kids to romp around many times thereafter.

WINTER TRIP

Most of the Christmases were spent with their Mom but on one occasion, I took them to Canada where my friend Gary had two children more or less the same ages (10 an 8) and had rented a house in the woods for Christmas, close to the skiing in the Laurentians…the kids had never skied…as a matter of fact, they had never seen SNOW!

As Gary and I drove thru the snow, you could feel the kid's excitement as we drove deeper into the woods. Gary finally found the driveway in the middle of nowhere. We told the kids to put on blindfolds and they did, laughing hysterically. As we entered the grounds surrounding the house, we got the kids out and while they were standing, Gary went over to the garage…ok, take off the blindfolds as Gary pulled on a switch and the entire house and trees lit up with Christmas lights…remember, my kids had never been in snow…OMG…snowball fights, angels in the snow, whooping and hollering in the winter wonderland…it was a sight to behold and remember…it was a great moment!!

Well, it was Christmas Eve and although we had a Christmas tree, we had no presents and I told the kids that there were to be no presents as the trip was the present and besides, Santa didn't even know where we were so forget about presents. They were cool with that.

Gary's kids had already had Christmas with their mother so there was no problem with them.

Everyone went to sleep and I sneaked out to my car where I had bought about thirty or forty gifts and hidden them way in the back behind the tire…it was f'n cold as I wrapped the gifts, and finally threw them under the tree, had a stiff drink to get warm and went to sleep.

I was awakened by the shouting from the four kids who woke everyone up 'Santa was here' they shouted. I said 'come on, let me sleep…there was no Santa and there is no presents, I told u last night!' 'No, no Santa came…come on, get up' they pulled the covers off me…'come on Daddy…he came, he came' as they tugged me down the stairs…and sure enough, Santa had come…and there were presents for everyone…the excitement was overwhelming as they all unwrapped the presents.

My brother Hank had taken me to learn to ski at North Conway, New Hampshire and Brattleboro, Vermont where you parked the car at the top of the mountain and skied down…anyway, I had skied Park City and Mammoth and was a pretty good skier.

In Canada we found a bunny hill to teach them the basics before putting them in ski school. I was able to show them how to put on the skis and how to walk on skis, what the fall line was and how to get up after falling by putting both skis up in the air and putting them downhill. I even taught them to snowplow or tried to... Nicolas thought he could just head downhill.

However, on this day he started to go down and fell into a snowdrift and couldn't move, or so he thought... and started to cry. I yelled 'put your skis up in the air '... nothing but more crying! I am not coming down there... put your skis in the air!" More crying!

Finally, he got one ski up...more crying...Jenna is laughing...more crying...second ski goes up in the air and he puts them down correctly and gets up...bravo!! Then they both manage to go down this 'baby slope' and they are now ready for school.

After several lessons, they could snowplow down the baby slopes and before you know it, they are skiing. Nicolas becomes an expert skier and Jenna is skiing at Sun Valley as I am writing this.

And that Christmas was one of the best of all time....

Fat Boy

My kids have always loved baseball. The summer I got divorced, I rented a beach house on Broad Beach in Malibu. I would never think of spending a summer with my kids not on a beach…anyway, I taught both my kids to hit and Nicolas would hit these monster shots onto the roof. We used wiffle balls and all the neighbors would come to watch the kid hit…he was 4.

Jenna could play as well and as soon as possible, I put them into whatever league would accept them…coach-pitch, t-ball…it didn't matter. I would coach them and we had fun.

Wherever we went for the summer, if possible, I would organize a summer league, get some t-shirts and we would play. Jenna would play on most of the teams.

When they reached Little League age, they went straight into majors, played for two years and eventually, they gave me a team.

Jenna was one of the first girls to play LL in Los Angeles.

Little League is a great bonding, father/child relationship builder that is good for everyone. They learn sportsmanship, competition, and how a team functions...its all good!

Its just that the Westwood LL and the West LA LL didn't speak to each other even though their fields were right next to each other with both right fields adjacent to the 405 Freeway. It's not if they didn't like each other... no, they hated each other!

They played the same game, had tryouts on the same day. Their coaches would line up along the right field dugouts just like the other league, holding the same pads to evaluate the kids for the coming draft...its just that they refused to talk to each other...a sort of Hatfields and McCoys in LA...go figure!

So, there I am at tryouts for the first time in the league. I'm given a pad with all the names of the new kids that have signed up. We each had a certain amount of players held over and we knew what we needed. I was the 'new' guy as most had managed the previous year.

The first group went out to left field and shagged balls and threw them toward home...then they were timed to 1st base...then they hit live pitching.

And we would evaluate them.

We had gone thru most of the kids and there were a few that stood out and many who could play the game... the last group trotted confidently out to left field.

As they were about to start the fly balls, I noticed an old pick-up truck and an Asian lady gets out with her stooped-over husband.

They motion for someone to get out and this big Asian kid appears and lumbers towards left field. No one knew who this was, but he had signed up. This was Tanaka. He was 12 years old, 5'7 and must have weighed 160lbs. He was big and awkward and didn't look coordinated at all!

The coaches are having a good laugh looking at this kid...'how can he play baseball', 'rather clothe him than feed him'...they giggle.

They hit him a fly ball and at the last minute he puts his glove hand down and backhands the ball then proceeds to throw it wildly toward home. The ball hits a fence and stops...he's a lefty thrower who has no clue. He can hardly run to 1ˢᵗ and he has no idea how to hit. The coaches sort of look at each other. It's all a bit embarrassing!

On Draft Night, everyone is there with their assistants and their good luck charms as the draft is about to begin…the 'New Guy' picks third.

So the first team picks the best player and the second guy ends up after consulting his 'crew', picking the second best player and then, all eyes are on the New-Guy.

The New-Guy says, 'Sorry guys, but the first half of this season is going to be miserable for you'…they all look at me…'what is this asshole going to say next!'

The New-Guy continues 'We probably wont lose a game in the 1st half'

…I pick Tanaka!

Everyone starts to shake their heads with total disregard…they think this is a joke… and finally laugh out loud…are you kidding!…"that fat boy cant play this game!".

You see, I saw things that Tanaka did that you couldn't teach…imagine the coordination to backhand a ball at your feet and then throw the ball out of the park…I also saw a left handed hitter that couldn't hit but IF HE COULD, he would hit the ball ONTO the 405!

I had been praying that no one saw what I saw…Look out League!

Well, I taught him how to pitch and he was unhittable…he threw the ball about 80+ MPH and no one could catch up to it…besides, he had an intimidating stare with a big leg kick before throwing.

No kid wanted to hit against him!

We won every game in the first half.

I also taught him to hit and in the first half, Tanaka hit not one but two balls onto the freeway behind right field. He became the best player in the league.

In the second half of the league, he was even better and we won going away!

But the best thing I ever did in Little League was to put the two leagues together. They said it couldn't be done but that just made me try harder and eventually, I figured it out…and they lived happily ever after.

The worst thing I did in Little League was not starting Tanaka in the 1st All-Star game and we lost on a fluke hit late in the game, so the world of Little League never saw the #1 pitcher in all of Little League that year!

Whenever I think of that game, I just shake my head.

Nickerson Housing Development AKA The Nick

It wasn't fair. There is no reason why there isn't a Little League team in Watts or Compton.

What's the matter…black kids can't play baseball!

God knows, they got talent, they just don't have the moola.

How much can it be? Uniforms for at least 4 teams, equipment for 4 teams and a fee to Little League…44 kids…hell, I can raise this little amount in my sleep! All I have to do is tell everyone what I am doing and the funds will appear…

So, I called Housing and then Parks and Rec to see which development had a baseball field…Nickerson fit the bill…so I went down there to meet the Parks and Rec guys.

Two smiling black guys just relaxing.

The first question out of there mouths was 'where did you park?'

I told them, as well as make and model and then I asked why?

White-boy, you in the Nick where there are forty-five... 45... crimes...hold it...hold it now...p e r- d a y!

I was stunned...but pressed on!

Well, can we have tryout to see if we can get 44 kids, 11and 12 year olds that want to play in the Little League?

They looked at each other..."Well, we can probably get more than half from the Nick but we will have problems getting kids from across that street (he pointed east) and that one (he pointed south).

Those blocks are 'Crip' blocks and we are in a 'Blood' block...Crip kids wont come into a Blood block to play anything period!"

I responded "Our only chance is to get permission from the Bloods to allow the 11s and 12s to cross the street. I'll tell you what. You organize the tryouts and I will organize the money and I will work with the coaches to help them teach and coach the kids. I'll also organize some equipment to be used during the tryouts…is that cool?"

They nodded and we shook hands and I left.

You know, I know a lot of people, and I know a lot of people that know a lot of people and would you believe it…I couldn't raise a dime!

Everyone said it was a lost cause and I should forget about it…I am talking to companies and very rich guys who turn down a budget of $3000 for a Little League…in 78'

I still don't understand it.

So I put it up, found equipment and uniforms and headed for the 'tryouts'

We were short the forty kids needed…they were stuck across the street!

I said to the rec guys 'Get the word to the Crips and Bloods that we have a Little League program set up… four teams of 14 kids and have uniforms, hats, bats and gloves and we want to play a 16 game season and we need your 11's and 12's to come and play…figure it out guys!

They just laughed and shooed me away!

The gangs did let their kids cross the street and we were able to fill out the teams and with some kid umps, so we started to play.

I coached the coaches and gave tips to players.

I got down to Nickerson several days a week just to see if it was still going on. Each day, when I saw everyone there, I was pleased and the league was a big success for the Nick…but the robberies just kept on going!

We had a party at the end of the season and over a beer I happened to say to the 'rec guys' that everything seemed to go rather smooth…and the 'rec guys' came unglued with laughter while pointing at me as they literally fell over!

Are you kidding us, do you have any idea how many brothers it took to make it seem like it was going 'smooth', as you put it!…they couldn't stop laughing.

We had two guys ready when you pulled up and one stayed to watch your car…the first guy was joined by another guy to make sure you got over here…safely!…that's 3.

Then another two would watch from the 1st base side and two more on the 3rd just to make sure that nothing happened to you during a game because you are 'loud'… that makes 7

Another two made sure you got back to your car… so, that means 9 guys each time you come down to the Nick!…but it was smooth!…they fell all over themselves!

I had no idea!

The 'rec guys' hugged me and thanked me for 'the effort' and hoped they could carry the program on but they realistically said it would be a problem…and it was!

The Little League lasted only one year but it was definitely worth it!

DMV

In the 70s' whenever you had a problem with your license or registration, you had to go to the Department of Motor Vehicles to get anything for the car. There was no internet or even computers or any way to get anything done except to go to the DMV.

So, there I was in line to get my license renewed and it was a long line. Even if you carefully figured out the best time to go, early or late or at lunchtime, it didn't matter…it was a long line. And this line went out the building and down the block, but, what the hell, you had to do it…

The line was moving ever so slowly as I had this whiff of 'Shalimar perfume'. I'd have to admit that this particular smell has always gotten to me and I wanted to know where it came from and it obviously came from the long-haired girl several places in front of me.

I don't know much about how other guys are attracted to women but I have always been a bit of a 'olfactory' nut and that particular smell has always gotten my attention! So, I just walked up to her and said something stupid like, how much I liked her perfume and she smiled and thanked me and that led to small talk about the perfume, the line, and other nonsensical bullshit and that led to her suggesting we meet for coffee and boom!... there you are.

It was the spring of 77'. Nicolas and Jenna were playing Little League in Westwood so at one point Alana, the girl from the DMV, suggested she wanted to see them play and so, she came and watched. Later I introduced them and we laughed a lot about something stupid and then she left. That night she couldn't get over the fact of how beautiful my kids were and that if she ever wanted a child, she would want me for the father…normally that would be a compliment but… as I looked at her she just laughed and then said that even if she wanted a child, she wanted nothing from me…just my name!

Little did I know that another Stern was on the way and at the end of the Little League Season, Alana announced she was pregnant and she was keeping the baby…if you knew Alana, you would know that that decision was 'final'.

Cameron Cash was brought up in Texas, graduated from the Univ. of Texas and has produced a film, acted in many and is the owner of his own Social Media Company as well as a dedicated Yogi.

He looks great and is enjoying a wonderful life in LA. He is my son and I am proud of him.

84'Olympics

In 1982, I was invited by the owners of Pax Productions to see the Beach Boys perform the first concert held after a baseball game, at Petco Park, home of the San Diego Padres.

It was Mothers Day and the sellout crowd waited in anticipation..

I had never been to San Diego and frankly, was in awe at the beauty of this part of California. This is the understatement of the year. I had been in Southern Cali for eighteen years and had never come down to one of the most beautiful beach areas in the world…and I am a beach-bum!…what a dummy!

I had a 'field-pass' and followed the production from outside the centerfield wall where the stage was built, to an area behind 2nd Base where the performance was to be held.

The Padres shot off fireworks to heighten the anticipation.

The stage was wheeled in and the Beach Boys came out to thunderous applause and played for close to two hours.

The baseball fans/Mothers all enjoyed the concert. It got great reviews and another concert was booked for the middle of the summer.

I was invited to the Pax office the next day to discuss the 'event'. I said that I loved the concert but I absolutely loved the concept of 'two for one'. See a game AND a concert!

They asked me if I would be willing to sell it to all the various sports franchises in the country. I said sure… it should be an easy sell…how do you get paid? And more important, how do I get paid? I need a guarantee amount per wk, travelling expenses and a taste of the profits, thinking like a producer. They said to meet in the morning and they would work it out…and they did!

Since I wasn't getting the acting parts I wanted, I jumped at the chance to sell to Major League Baseball. Being crazy about baseball helped and selling was a challenge I loved.

They rented me a house for three months in Solana Beach and living with a view of the ocean made me realize how much I missed the ocean...

Pax was only ready to do concerts on the West Coast so we were limited to the teams in LA, SF, and Seattle... my first 'pitch' was to the head of marketing at the San Francisco Giants, Pat Gallager. He was intrigued with the 2 for 1 concept and became our 2nd concert.

This was very successful and we booked another with them so, we had 2 in San Diego and 2 in SF. This made selling even easier, so I sold Seattle on a concert and started to open up the next closest teams...namely Denver and then I sold Portland whose sport was soccer. That concluded the first baseball season.

I brought the kids down to Solana Beach for the summer and they fell in love with the beaches of North County.

The following summer I got Nicolas his first entertainment job, picking up the talent at the various airports and being a sort of production assistant. He ended up running the show several years later.

(Before that Nicolas had worked as an assistant to a chef at a very 'posh' restaurant near my place on Rangely.)

The concert business had tripled as I sold everybody this 'new' concept.

In the summer of 83' Samantha and I agreed that the cost of Crossroads was becoming a problem and I voiced my desire to have the kids live with me in North County for their two remaining years in high school...Nicolas wanted to live with me but Jenna didn't want to leave her friends. She reluctantly agreed.

I had to find the 'right' school for them. As I looked at the various high schools, one stood out. Its probably hard to understand but in 83' there were no houses or anything else east of the 5 freeway...nothing was there except a set of unusual buildings up on a hill that looked like a Buckminster Fuller design (a famous ultra-modern architect of the period).

As I drove up the only road to the buildings, I was blown away by the design...the most beautiful high school I had ever seen...the students ate lunch with an ocean view...slightly better looking than Asbury Park high School!

I wondered if the volleyball coach had an opening at 'setter'...I had to find something that Jenna would love... so that maybe she would at least talk to me... I called him and asked if he would meet me for coffee...I had a daughter that loved to play volleyball and I was trying to find the right school. He agreed to meet.

A very nice young coach met me…I have only one question for you, I said…is the setter position open for competition? I held my breath as he looked at me 'the father', smiled and said yes, it is open. I breathed a sigh of relief!

He then asked about Jenna and I told him that she was good and needed to compete…I then told him about my looking for the right 'fit' and I loved the look of Torrey Pines. I really liked this guy and kept my fingers crossed that Jenna might like him and TP.

The kids moved down to a house I rented on Nogales in Del Mar…Jenna didn't talk to me but she did try out for volleyball. When the first practice ended, I got a call from the coach…thanking me for bringing Jenna, and added that I was the first father to ever tell him the truth about their kid.

The volleyball team had a small following until Nicolas started a cheering section of boys who dressed differently for each game and they brought in a large following for the girls team…Jenna said that the people were coming to see Nicolas' cheering squad in dresses cheering the girls…it was quite a site!

Jenna played for two years and made first team All San Diego which would lead to her being accepted at UC Berkley where she promptly gave up volleyball for 'Asian Studies and Drama'.

The house became 'the house' for all their friends. Nicolas and Jenna were 'the new kids' but they were friendly, and their dad was cool so…partee!!

I was still selling concerts and one is notable… Cleveland… where we got Crosby, Stills and Nash to play. I flew out to Cleveland, Nicolas didn't go on this one… he had school!

Crosby was addicted to cocaine and had had quite a bit before leaving his dressing room. On the way out to the stage, he did a face plant into the Cleveland outfield…lying face down, he was picked up by a couple of stagehands and taken up the stairs and stood up in front of the mike as the crew put his guitar over his neck and left him there…I honestly thought he was unconscious but he never missed a beat…played flawlessly!

As they were taking him up the stairs, a production assistant rushes up to me to tell me I had a call…

So?

Its from a sheriff…

Yes sir, this is Tom Stern

This is the Del Mar sheriff…your son has been arrested and we are holding him here.

In jail?

'Serving liquor to minors'…I thought for a moment… this could have been me!

'What would you like us to do sir?'

Pause

'Well, just leave him!…there is nothing I can do from Cleveland!…

He's a big boy, he can take care of himself'

Call you back in two hrs…bye…and when I finally called, they had kept him for several hours and drove him home.. I am sure the partee was still on!!

SURFING
I had always been attracted to surfing because it was a water sport and I was a fish…from NJ, but there had

never been surfing while I was growing up (until Endless Summer came out, there was no surfing on boards) but I felt totally comfortable in the ocean, riding the biggest waves ...bodysurfing!

So when I passed the surfing breaks at Cardiff Beach and Swami's, I knew that somehow I was going to learn this sport as it looked sooooo fun!!

Every chance I got, I tried to learn to surf...in case you don't know, Surfing has the longest learning curve in all of sports...so I got a 7' board and started paying dues...I couldn't even get up until someone switched boards with me, his being an 8'6". I had never gotten up, without falling...but the minute I got on the 8'6, my life changed forever.

NOTE: every sport had always come easy to me until I attempted surfing. While in LA around 68', I had gone down to Malibu, thinking that like all other sports, it will come easy and since I grew up in the ocean, big waves didn't bother me. So I rented a short-board and with towel thrown over the board 'the right way', sauntered down to the water, thinking I would just get on it, paddle out and surf.

No one had told me about 'wax', so when I jumped on the board and fell off...attempting this a number of times...I heard this laughter coming from the sunbathers and thought nothing of it until I realized it was about the dummy trying to surf without wax…duh!…left the beach, embarrassed as hell, and never touched a board till twelve years later in Solana Beach.

Needless to say, I loved living with the kids and I think they loved being with their crazy dad.

A NOTE FROM JENNA:
"You were asking me what I remember of San Diego in the early 80s. Many images come to mind but here is what comes up first:

> You had been going down there and falling in love with the place. The rooms and then houses that you had were always fun to visit. The house in Solana Beach was on a hill and had a great deck overlooking the water. The little house in Encinitas next to the farms was pretty cool too. They felt like vacation houses…cottages… it was fun to come down and stay there with you on the weekends.

> When you and mom then decided to have Nicolas and I come down to live with you the following year, you moved again. You found the best school in the area and a house in that school district. I remember you were still just learning to

surf and you had your longboard and a full head of white hair and all the locals thought you were some old timer with your longboard, and gave you all the waves!

Lucky.

Maybe that should be the title of this book... lucky :-)

Lucky strike lucky guy lucky to get the waves, lucky getting the girls and lucky us .., to have you as our dad.

Xoxo
Jenna"

Peeeeench!!

When Nicolas graduated from Torrey Pines, he was accepted to Utah (U of U) and he decided to live in Park City naturally, so he could ski his ass off and occasionally attend class…a bit of a 'chip off the old block' so to speak…

Jenna, on the other hand thoroughly enjoyed academia and was accepted to UC Berkeley…I thought she would play volleyball because as an All-Star she was really good but as soon as she arrived at school, she had other thoughts in mind…oh, what a surprise…not!

The next thing I knew, she was in a play and had enrolled in 'Asian Studies' so she was going to be an actress?…in Japan?…are you kidding me!

I had never seen Jenna in any form of a play before, so I was a bit shocked to be invited to see her in a Bertolt Brecht play. Naturally I went up to Berkeley to see her.

I didn't realize it at the time but Brecht had written this esoteric play as a musical and sure enough, Jenna appeared and sang…not only had I not seen her in a play but I had never even dreamed she could sing…as soon as I dried my tears, I realized that she was truly talented…

It was so obvious, I missed it completely…she was the daughter of an accomplished actress (now referred to as 'actor') and an actor, so why shouldn't she do it all….

So in her junior year, since she was majoring in Asian Studies with a minor in Drama, she decided to go to Japan and study at a well-known university in Mitaka, just outside of Tokyo.

One part of the program was to visit families during the holidays and Jenna was all-in for that. The family she visited over New Years was in Kyushu in the southern section of Japan. The father was a Buddhist Priest and they lived in the compound of the temple.

She really enjoyed the experience, so when I decided to take Nicolas over to Japan to see Jenna and then take them both to Thailand, one of the things Jenna wanted us to do was visit her Homestay Family…so we did.

Jenna had planned the Tokyo part of our trip including famous shrines as well as Shibuya, the famous 'youth hangout' Roppongi and Harajuku, famous for it's youth-oriented shopping. She took us everywhere eating sushi and soaking up the 'new' environment…the Tokyo train station, Shinjuku, was a revelation, as it reminded me of an 'ant-hill'…thousands of commuters scurrying in all directions all at the same time…unbelievable sight!

We went to several Shrines and the town of Mitaka was an interesting contrast to our normal lives…we then headed to Kyushu on the high-speed train which is the 'only way to travel'…

We arrived around 5pm and were met by the Priest, a small, rather chubby fellow…accompanied by a giant man who looked like 'Odd Jobs', a 'James Bond' bad guy…he was bald and carried a key-chain filled with keys. You wouldn't want to meet him in a dark alley!

They both had radiant smiles and greeted Jenna like a long-lost daughter…they obviously loved her. Of course Jenna spoke Japanese to them and we just nodded and smiled..

We all piled into a van, with the 'big guy' driving and headed to 'the Shrine' which turned out to be an ornate temple with living quarters attached and the Priest himself showed us to our quarters which were very nice… he told us that the 'dinner meal' would be ready in thirty minutes.

We didn't know what to wear until Jenna told us it would be 'informal' and not to worry.

I knew nothing about the Priest, but I knew the Japanese loved to drink...and their favorite was scotch-whiskey, so I brought two bottles of Pinch, a high-end scotch whisky as a gift...I had to bring a gift!

So, in thirty minutes we descended the stairs and entered the dining room...we were stunned!...there was a very long table filled with people, various dishes and many ladies serving.

The priest introduced everyone in broken English... the Mayor and his wife, the Police Chief and his wife, the Fire Marshal and his wife, the Head of the Town Council and his wife, the Mayor's assistant, the Police Chief's assistant, the Fire Marshal's assistant and all of us...the table was filled and I was given the seat at the head of the table and the Priest was at the other end.

There had to have been twenty ladies all preparing food and the feast started...as the first course was served, I took out a bottle of scotch and held it up to the Priest and a chorus of PEEEEEENCH!! rang out...they all knew the beautifully designed bottle of Scotch whiskey...it was passed around and the sake glasses were filled with the scotch whiskey.

A thinly sliced course of fillet mignon and the many veggies cooked Japanese style were served and there was much toasting to me and Jenna and Nicolas and at the height of laughter and merriment, as course after course was served, and just after the main course was served amid much laughter and toasting, I took out the second bottle of scotch and held it up…

PEEEEEEEEENCH drowned out any other conversation as the Japanese hooted and hollered as the scotch was again passed around.
Everyone was having a wonderful time drinking, eating and toasting when suddenly…

The Mayor did a face-plant into his plate of food…the laughter continued as if this was a regular occurrence… the Mayor's wife did a similar face-plant into her food!!

Then the Fire Chief did a face-plant into his food followed by his wife…I mean people were face-planting right and left…and they just left them there… faces in the plates of meat and veggies and rice…

The women couldn't clear the gigantic table because all the officials and their wives were passed out on the plates of food…

The kids had left as the bowling pins were going down all over the place…Finally I proposed a toast to the Priest

JUST LUCKY I GUESS

and as we raised our glasses, we noticed we were the only ones still standing and he started to toast in English... talk about a crazy time!!!

As the Priest appeared about ready to pass out, Odd Jobs tapped me on the shoulder and motioned me to come with him...I looked at the Priest and he nodded so I left with the big guy!

To this day I don't know how we communicated but we did. He drove to some obscure looking building and motioned me to follow. He pulled out his huge ring of keys and moved them around and found the one he was looking for and opened the door...

I couldn't believe what I was watching...it was a bar crowded with men drinking...all men...several men got up to give Odd Jobs two seats at the bar...he ordered and it was as if he had told a joke...much laughter as everyone looked at me...uh oh...now what!!

While sipping a beer (you know I am not much of a drinker) a waiter came out of the back holding a tray with a bowl on it. As he worked his way down the bar, there was much laughter as everyone turned and looked at me. This was really funny...to them!

The waiter served a bowl of soup and put it down in front of me as all eyes were on me...I looked at Odd Jobs and he pointed to the soup...IT WAS ALIVE!!...holy shit, it was bubbling…all these fucks wanted to see if the American had the balls to drink the soup…they were cheering and banging on the bar in unison…they had done this before!!

I looked up at Odd Jobs who was smiling and picked up the bowl. I downed it in several gulps…the place went nuts!! Odd Jobs gave me a thumbs up and we left to thunderous applause.

We went to several other bars and he just let himself in and then he took me to a beautiful house…of ill repute…

The next day Nicolas and I took a walk thru the neighborhood and as we passed a school, I noticed all the kids at the windows looking at us.

Suddenly, the windows opened and the kids started jumping out and running towards us…now that was strange…they spoke broken English and asked 'Are you Americans' and we nodded as more students jumped out the windows…we had a crowd of students firing questions at us. Nicolas answered their questions and I answered as well and after what seemed like a long time, we told them that they should go back to school as we had to go. Reluctantly they turned and went back continuing to look over their shoulders. Amazing!!

Well, we left Kyushu and headed back to Mitaka, stayed overnight and headed for the airport on our way to the warm sunny beach town of Phuket with an overnight in Bangkok.

In Bangkok, we went out to dinner at a restaurant where you picked the 'live' food you were about to eat... very strange I must admit...after dinner, Jenna was exhausted from being the 'tour director', so she went to sleep and I took Nicolas out to see the town.

The next day we left for Phuket and arrived around 3pm to find an empty town...no one was out as the 'siesta' was being observed or so we thought. We got to the small hotel on the beach and we immediately headed for the water which was so hot, it was difficult to go in...the water felt like a it was 100 degrees and it was definitely over 90 on land...so the only way to get refreshed was to go in, so when you got out, it felt cool...not good!

I never checked the water temp so I was at fault here... anyway, we went out to eat around 6pm and you wouldn't believe how crowded it was. You couldn't walk in the town...that's how crowded it was.

The next day the kids wanted to see the other islands and I wanted to just sleep and laze around in and around the water, getting the usual massage on the beach and eating the local 'stands' in town. We could only take the heat for so long so after four days we left, going back to Bangkok where Jenna would head back to Tokyo and we headed to Hong Kong as our final stopover to returning to the states.

You cant go to Hong Kong without visiting the 'overnight tailors' that churn out the finest suits, ties and shoes in a blink…from scratch. Naturally, I introduced Nicolas to the finer cuts and styles of the times. Remember, my brother worked in the Textile Industry and I became aware of all the best fabrics for suits, ties and shirts. In addition my brother's boss, Lou Bachman, introduced me to gourmet foods, fine dining and good cigars. He gave me my 'champagne tastes with a beer budget'.

Anyway, Nicolas and I came back to the States with a 'proper' wardrobe for the gentlemen we were…suits, shirts, shoes etc…a great time had by all…PEEEENCH!!

Fire on the Beach

It was the winter of 85' and I had just gotten out of the water and it was freezing. My buddy with the brandy was nowhere to be found and I was fucking cold! I spotted a fire on the beach down the way and I immediately headed for it.

There was a girl all huddled up in a chair and I wasn't the only guy to notice a fire…it was crowded with ogling guys but I came up and started to get my hands warm and I noticed the 'huddled girl' and as she looked at me she smiled and I noticed this incredible smile was on a stunning face!

Ok, guys and girls, there are many things that attract a guy to a girl…it could be anything from their upper bodies to their rear end or any number of things such as their hands or their eyes or their hair or their legs or their voice but in the long run you had better love their face because that is what you will have to look at the most!

And this girl had a face that you would never get tired of looking at...I didn't know a thing about her but I loved what she looked like and she offered me a 'Kahlua and coffee' which I took immediately even though I don't drink...maybe it will make me warm...and it did!

When a surfer comes out of very cold water, he or she will drink anything hot...it could be poison but they would drink it right down...if it were HOT!

Anyway, I watched as the guys hit on her and eventually they all left and I returned and introduced myself and met Nancy Fisher. She is with me today, but not without some turmoil.

Lets see, Nancy is the smartest lady I have ever known but she had no concept of a Jewish guy with a sarcastic sense of humor...she thought I was serious all the time and of course I was just kidding around.

I guess coming from a large family of four brothers and two sisters, being Catholic and having a Dad who was a Commander in the Navy (this rank is the same as a Brigadier General in the Army) left her a bit confused, humor wise and frankly, I had never dated or hung out with anyone like her before.

Normally I would have run from anyone like Nancy, but there I was!

I loved good food, Nancy liked 'fast food'...I didn't drink, Nancy did...I didn't smoke and disliked girls that smoked and Nancy smoked...I hated horses and of course Nancy loved them and has had one for as long as I can remember...you get the drift!

I like meat rare and Nancy likes it well done I am right-handed and Nancy is left-handed Nancy has long wavy dark hair and I have super-curly white hair...the list goes on and on but I wont bore you.

After an on and off again relationship, Nancy invited me to Thanksgiving.

Now, you have got to realize what a giant step this was for Nancy...at the time, I didn't realize it, but this was a BIG deal!

I didn't know a single member of her rather large family and they were ALL going to be there...a brother from Philadelphia with wife and two children...a brother from Vermont with wife...a brother from San Diego with wife and two children...a sister from around the corner with husband and two children...another sister (who is now deceased) and a brother from San Diego and Nancy.

I thought to myself that Alice, her poor mother, must have been pregnant for ten years...Nancy's Dad, a Commander in the Navy was assigned a different command every two to three years and they have lived everywhere or so it seems...you name a place and someone was either conceived there or born there!

You all know Thanksgiving...no one sits down on time and especially if you have as many moving parts as this family has. In my family, if we sat down an hour late, that would be the norm.

Anyway I was driving up the coast in my van and I happened to pass a great surf break called County Line and they had some rideable waves, so I stopped, looked at my watch and figured out that I would be about 15min late which in my mind was perfect!

Rode the waves for about 30min and headed to Nancy's mothers house and arrived to find them... all sitting down and eating...OMG!!...I got the dreaded stare from Nancy but everyone else seemed to be ok...headed for the Commander, who I immediately liked...a real no nonsense guy who looked you in the eye when he talked to you...and I knew he liked me by the way he handled my being late!

'Alice, if he wanted to be on time, he would have been here, now lets eat!'

I immediately knew he loved Nancy because she took no crap from any of her brothers or sisters…he just laughed at her…they definitely had a bond.

And her mother was a 'pistol' as well…I had been warned that I might get something thrown at me for 'bad language' and sure enough, here came a flying napkin because of something I said…Alice is a great lady!

Ok, dinner was over and one of the brothers said to me 'do you play basketball?' Cause we always play 'horse' after our Thanksgiving meal so we can get ready to eat dessert!

I play 'a little' I said and you could see all of them nod at each other…'we got us one here boys'

The brothers were all nice guys and they were all into sports so they could shoot but they kind of underestimated the new guy. We had a good time…actually, they were ok but they talked a good game till I started to shoot left handed and then they were done.

Nancy worked for banks in the real estate/mortgage lending division which I knew absolutely nothing about and it seemed as if all her bosses were impossible to deal with and treated her badly as well.

This was not good for me because I wanted to straighten them out, so to speak!...Nancy just took it and pressed onward, just doing her job which was a case of overwork and underpay...they took unreasonable advantage of her and it pissed me off but that's the way it was/is.

Of course, Nancy knew nothing about the film biz but then again, why should she?...so here we were, deciding to live together but not knowing anything about the other's work.

We found a great house in Cardiff and have lived together since the late 90s'.

As I write this I realize I am about to ask Nancy to marry me and will ask her on her 65th birthday as I take her out for dinner on Nov 7th at Vigalucci's...its our secret so don't tell her ok? I am going to give her an antique ring and 'take a knee"...if she turns me down, I will let u know...

Note: She didn't and we got married on Jan 13, 2018 in Nicolas's backyard, in front of a small group of friends and family.

Da Big Board Break

When I started to surf, of course I knew nothing about the sport other than I was totally comfortable in the ocean, having been brought up a 'summer beach boy' at the Jersey Shore. My father had taught me how to ride waves on my belly and I was not intimidated by the ocean. Body surfing teaches you a healthy respect for all the different currents and weather as it affects the waves, so I was way ahead of the curve when it came to learning to surf…that is to say I was not afraid of big waves!

NOTE: there was no surfing when I was growing up… in fact, the east coast never knew anything about surfing till 'Endless Summer' came out in June 1966.

The day my friend made me ride his 8'6 board, I was 50 years old and it was the defining moment in the impossible 'learning curve' of surfing, which is the hardest in all of sports…it takes a long time to learn to surf properly.

I immediately went out and bought a 9'0 board and got up on any wave I was able to catch. But I had to learn the 'pecking order' so that the 'enforcer' who is at every 'break' didn't come up to me and tell me to 'get out of the water bro'…you're a menace!

Once you get up easily, you can improve rapidly assuming you don't think you know it all and ask guidance whenever you are 'over your head' which happens on a daily basis.

I immediately realized that I didn't like 'sitting in the pack' hearing all the family-social banter of the moment, so I learned to go out further than anyone and just wait for the biggest wave in the set of three or four waves.

That became my M.O. (modus operandi) for my surfing life…go out the furthest and catch the biggest wave!

Even though I liked to be alone out in the ocean, I knew every surfer from Cardiff to Swami's and enjoyed the sport more than I ever imagined. In fact, I forgot softball for the first twelve years I was in Cardiff…never knew about the league I now play in!

I find that incredible, because I played ball all my life! But surfing took over my brain.

So, I would work in LA and come down for the long weekend to surf. I eventually rented a room in Denny Martin's house and went back and forth for a number of years. Denny was one of the best surfers on the West Coast and one of the nicest guys you could hope to meet. While he was surfing, however, you couldn't talk to him at all. He was totally consumed, moving in and out relentlessly challenging the waves. I called him 'motorman' as he never stopped!

I was 'crazy' about surfing and as soon as possible each week, I would leave LA for Cardiff. My life centered around the waves. One day I read about these guys in Maui riding 70ft waves and immediately thought of making a film with these huge waves as the background…not a documentary but a feature film. I started to write ideas down…there I was, in my van, writing on yellow pads (we did that back in the day)…thinking of doing a film that nobody had done before, got my juices flowing.

After all, I had done the first motorcycle film that a family could see (Hells Angels 69), one of the first films on Vietnam (Clay Pigeon), the first large soccer film (Victory)…why not big-wave surfing?

There were many, many 16mm films made every year, but never a big 35mm film and that's what I wanted to do…I thought of a story of four big-wave riders going to the biggest waves on the planet starting from LA going to South Africa thru Brazil and then to Bali and ending in Hawaii.

(NOTE: no matter what story you can think of, if it involves going from one place to another, you risk comparison with the one and only 'Endless Summer' but I thought the big-wave aspect would carry me.)

While in Rio de Janeiro, Brazil, at a party given for our four surfers, a large jewel robbery takes place and the jewels find their way, inadvertently, to the host, who hides them in a surfboard (he used to smuggle drugs into Brazil this way) and when he is invited to join the 'group' headed to Africa, (the host is also a big-wave rider) he brings several boards including 'the one'.

The bad guys soon follow and the chase begins without the surfers knowing anything till they reach Hawaii where all hell breaks loose…

Finally I finish the screenplay and called it 'Forces of Nature'.

When trying to sell a screenplay, you try to find the 'right' guy to pitch it too…then it's a short and quick… yes or no!!

My first 'pitch' was to David Saunders at Triumph Productions at Columbia Pictures and my pitch was short and sweet...all I said was 'that I wanted to tell a story about surfers that surf 80ft waves'...and of course he didn't believe me but he said he would read the screenplay.

A few days later he called and said that the screenplay was alright, but someone had to prove to the studios that these guys existed. I'll get you some money and you prove it!!...go out and film waves...big ones!!

I love challenges...

Some money proved to be $200,000 (remember, I only had 250 thou to do my first film HA 69 and here they give me 200 just to go out and film) and the first person I contacted was Paul Strauch, the Hawaiian legend who I needed, in order to get to the guys on a proper basis... we went to Hawaii and to Maui to talk to the only guys at the time that surfed 'Jaws', one of the biggest surf breaks on the planet.

We made a deal to film the next 'very large swell' and I would teach the local filmmakers how to use a 35mm cameras, which were larger and heavier than the little 16mm they were used to.

Paul and I went to Hawaii and rented a house on Kawela Bay, where we could both paddle out and surf the waves of the North Shore. While there, we organized two crews to film both on the North Shore of Oahu and Jaws on Maui and waited... and waited...

As Lefty Gomez used to say 'its better to be lucky than good' and wouldn't you know it...the largest storm in years came in to Hawaii...an unbelievable 'storm from hell' with no wind!... creating 60-80ft waves on Jaws and 20-30ft in Oahu...so in one day, I brought back to Columbia three hours of these giant waves...they were positively blown away! They had never seen anything like it!

The problem was that every director that saw these waves wanted to do a film with the waves but...I owned the footage and I wanted to direct the film.

Saunders had me over the barrel by saying that the 'decision makers' didn't like my screenplay but would pay me all the fees (directors fee plus the producer's fee and the writers fee) but someone else was going to direct a film, (not mine) using these waves!

Reluctantly, I agreed and Saunders gave the film to Zalman King, his partner (oh, what a surprise)...and then I had to fight to keep the big waves in the film...

aint the business grand! (BTW, Zalman used to be the lifeguard at the Ocean Beach Club in Jersey!)

Well, right in the middle of the shoot, David Saunders gets fired…In 'Hollywood', when a guy gets fired, all the films associated with him get thrown in the 'toilet', so to speak…

So when it was all over, I went to the highest ranking Distribution Exec VP and asked for a small favor, considering he was about to 'tank' the film…

He said 'what do you want?'

I want to use the film for charity…I'll play it in Hawaii, San Diego and Los Angeles and then it is all yours…he agreed.

I premiered the film in Hawaii and raised the entire budget of the 'Junior Lifeguard Program' for all the islands…after all, the film was about the giant waves at Jaws and the Hawaiians loved it…

An 11ft board signed by the Hawaiian legend Buffalo Keaulana was raffled off…everyone wanted the board but the Hawaiians loved me for doing the premiere in Honolulu and kinda made sure I won the board which was frankly, a shock to me…

Then I premiered the film in San Diego for 'Inner City Kids' and raised close to $20,000 for them...

I also raised another $15,000 for Surfrider in the LA premiere.

We did so well in all three cities, Sony asked me where in the US did I feel the film would do well and I answered 'Oklahoma City' because they had never seen anything like this...

Naturally, they took the film to Florida where it 'tanked'...and that was that...

I started to ride the 11ft board and there were no waves in the Southern California area that were too big for that board...and it was effortless...it just glided along catching everything...until one day at Swami's, I was way outside and I saw the kelp bed move, so I started to paddle out...a huge 20+ ft wave came and I turned and paddled and caught it, started down and ...it rose up and spit me away and as if I was a fly...when I finally made my way to the surface, my board was in two pieces...it had died an heroic death...

Several years later, arthritis in my right shoulder stopped me in my tracks...I couldn't paddle...but I have no complaints as I surfed for over 30 years...a good run in any sport!

Sundays

One day at the beach, I saw this guy coming up the stairs, carrying his board…his name was Pat Steel and he was a great surfer, his wife Betty, a surfer as well, sold real estate.

I said, Pat, I hear you play softball?

He said yeah, do you play?

I said yeah, I play a little…

Pat said do you want to hit some time?

(Here we go again…he just wants to see if I can play…at all!…he doesn't want to take me to his league if I cant play, right?)

I said yeah, I'd love to!

Well, I got some balls and a couple of bats in my car… maybe tomorrow…I know a place where we could go…

So the next day we went to this field that I am sure was never used for baseball, although they had a backstop and a bunch of trees in right field and a left field that doubled as a football field…(Pat's thinking: no one will see him just incase he cant play at all)

Pat said how do you bat?

I bat lefty, I said…oh, okay…I'll pitch you some…(you could see his brain working)

Hadn't swung a bat in awhile…came down to Cardiff in 85' and hadn't picked up a bat since then…it was now 1999….14yrs…wow! that's the longest I have been without baseball in my life…surfing must be a spectacular sport!!

Anyway, I picked up the bat and swung it a few times and it felt like I hadn't missed a day…so Pat pitched underhand and the first ball I hit went over the trees into the street.

Pat just stood there like he couldn't believe it…

So he pitched another and the same thing happened...boom over the trees..

Pat said 'well, you sure can hit'...where you been hiding?

Right in front of your eyes, surfing at Barney's...just forgot how much I miss baseball, then I heard you played so I thought I'd ask...

Pat said 'glad you did'.

Do you want to play in the league I play in...I nod... cause the guys there are going to love you...I don't think you can play on my team, but I know they will find you a team!

PAT STEEL'S ACCOUNT
If I give myself an unbiased opinion of my personality, I would have to admit to being anti-social. I'm not interested in the trivial banter with strangers.

Years ago I was standing on a bluff checking the surf out, the waves were good size and crowded. I had my eye on a fickle sandbar that was dependent on tide and had a small window of being rideable. The attraction was it was uncrowded even though it was in plain view of two crowded reef breaks.

My concentrated diagnosis was interrupted by a white haired older gentleman, Tom Stern, who asked, "what do you think is the best place to go out?". I quickly sized him up as not a threat to compete for waves at my secret spot. " I'm going out right there and pointed to a spot that didn't even look like a surf break. "It will be good in a half hour when the tide goes out."

A half hour later I paddled out and to my surprise Tom was already sitting in the spot I pointed to. Sure enough with the tide lower the waves were good with only Tom and I riding them. Eventually the wave of the day came and with Tom on a longboard and I being on a shortboard, he out paddled me to position.

There he was riding past me on a beautiful overhead wave that lasted forever. I was cursing myself for giving him my inside information on a place I had studied for years. I was also cursing him, this stranger who stole my wave.

Eventually I forgave him; it's impossible to stay mad at Tom.

Over the next few months we became friends. Eventually he discovered one of my other passions, softball. We both had played a lot of baseball in our lives. I was playing in a couple of softball leagues. At one time softballs were soft, now they are like a giant baseball and hard as rocks.

Tom kept pestering me to go hit with him. I am unfortunately very competitive and didn't want to waste my time with him. If you know Tom, you know he is persistent. I eventually agreed to go hit with him.

I took him to a park that had a lower girls field and an upper men's field. Since I didn't expect much we hit on the girls field. We warmed up with a game of catch. As I expected his throws were weak and I wrote him off as a has been. He told me he had injured his shoulder and had difficulty throwing. Yeah, sure.

When I pitched to him he batted left handed. He had a nice swing but nothing unusual. He whacked his fourth pitch deep, I turned to watch the flight. The ball sailed over the fence, over the embankment and over the fence on the upper field. Whoa that was a lucky shot.

When he deposited the next ten balls in the same place I realized luck had nothing to do with it. This guy can hit!

I got him on one of my teams. It was hilarious to watch the teams move their outfield in when they saw him come up. Every game he burned them by hitting balls over their heads. It took two seasons before they gave him the respect he deserved. Even then he would launch a bomb over their heads.

Tom has reached legendary status in the league. The annual Home Run Derby is now named after him. I'm grateful that I took the time to give Tom a chance to show his abilities. He inspires me.

• • •

So, in 1999, I started to play in the La Costa Canyon Athletic League…LCC for short.

The word got around pretty fast…Pat had brought this new guy into the league and he can pound the ball!
But of course nobody believed him.

There is a natural phenomenon that takes place in all leagues when an 'older guy' enters the league. They play him in accordance with his age, that is to say 'without respect'

No one believes the 'older guy' can hit, so when I hit it over the outfielder's head or bounce it over the fence, it just a 'fluke' and they don't change their position on the field...well, this happened each game and I would hit it over their heads or bounce it out for a triple and they just could not believe their eyes. One game I had five triples and the next game, they were in the same position...oh well!

LIKE NO OTHER
San Diego and California in general is a place that you can play any sport every day of the year...whatever the sport, there is a league going or a place that is devoted to playing that sport. You just have to figure out the 'where' and you can play every day...but I don't care what sport you play, there is nothing in this world like LCC...at least for me!

Since the first day I played at LCC, I have been the oldest player in the league and I have always played in both divisions that play only on Sunday...a 55 and over and a 35 and over divisions.

I have always loved to hit! So playing in both divisions allowed me to get up to the plate around 8 times every Sun.

When I tell people that we are a '3 pitch, pitch to yourself league' and the only one like it in the country, everyone is perplexed.

'You pitch to yourself?'…each team supplies the pitcher and the other team has 10 players playing…5 infielders and 4 outfielders and the catcher…the hitting team supplies the pitcher and the hitter is allowed 3 pitches only!

Seems too easy at first…but there are 9 guys fielding, not 7 that you see on your TV screens at home…also, you only get 3 pitches and can only get another pitch if you hit the screen protecting the pitcher.

Every team makes the playoffs and a balancing committee makes sure the teams are balanced…Ok, that's the game we play but the league is so much more than that!

The guys bring their families and one of the better players in the league (Jack) also cooks so every week there is food for all.

And of course everyone drinks beer…it's the ultimate 'beer' league…

We all look forward to Sundays…we all make fun of each other and laughter is heard thru out the day…its like no other league any of us has ever played in.

My second year in the league, I went up to the manager of YMI, Leo Benavidez, and told him that I wanted to be on the same team as Pat, who brought me into the league. I stayed on YMI older and younger teams for 12yrs and enjoyed every minute.

For my 75th birthday, Nancy and I were going to Leo's house for a quiet dinner…I was making a salad as my contribution.

As I came around the corner of the house, there stood at least fifty guys in tuxedos screaming happy birthday and other things.

Jenna had come from NYC and Nicolas from LA and there had to be at least one-hundred friends from everywhere…of course Nancy pulled off the 'con'…they even had a tux for me to change into…it was a great and only surprise party I had ever had…the best!

All I know is that every Sun, when I arrive at the field, I get this overwhelming feeling of a kind of love that can only come from a bunch of beer-drinking ball players that just happen to like you.

To Be Continued

After going thru the various stories, I realize that although my stories are unique to me, they made me realize that you have a book of short stories just waiting for you to write them.

Consider this book as a 'teachable moment' confirming for you the possibility that I may be right. That you too have several titles that you might take a shot at writing. Great!

We are entering 2018 and the whole world is changing at a rapid pace. As you must have realized, I have always loved women and we are beginning to realize that they will eventually take over most of the 'power' positions that men have had and screwed up over time.

It will be interesting to see what they do with their power. They are definitely the best thing put on this planet and I am sure the world will be a better place with them running the show!

Speaking of power, Ros always instilled in me the idea that I could do anything I wanted to do…she instilled the idea that although we weren't wealthy, we were rich in love and family values. She was a very positive woman.

My life has always felt quite blessed in that I actually felt that I could get whatever came my way, done, even when the odds were against me…so you might guess that the word 'no' was not easily accepted.

Having been given outstanding 'hand/eye coordination' only contributed to my positive outlook on life…I never considered the negative as absolute…it just meant that I had to re-evaluate the situation and find another way to get a positive response.

My teen years were affected by older experienced men that somehow took a liking to the 'wiseguy-kid' that actually made fun of them…with that grin all over his face.

Note: when I came back from 'soldiering', I got job offers from all of them from Hess Oil to Baer-Stearns on Wall Street…I was given advice from Sonny Werblin who founded what became Universal Pictures…he told me to never go into showbiz! You can see how I took that advice!

Ros and Harry brought me up to make my own decisions and from about seventeen, I did just that. I put myself thru college and became a very independent happy soul…which translated into trying everything that I thought would contribute to my positive outlook on life…

Thats all for now. Thanks for reading.

Now… START WRITING DOWN TITLES…

I AM WAITING TO READ YOURS.

***** SPECIAL THANKS TO MY DAUGHTER JENNA FOR HER HELP WITH DESIGN AND EDITORIAL…COULDN'T HAVE FINISHED THIS WITHOUT HER…LOVE YOU FOREVER.

(Love you too, Papa! xoxo)

Made in the USA
San Bernardino, CA
23 March 2018